Public Reaction to Supreme Court Decisions

In *Public Reaction to Supreme Court Decisions*, Valerie Hoekstra looks at reactions to Supreme Court decisions in the local communities where the controversies began. She finds considerable media coverage of these cases and a highly informed local populace. While the rulings did not have a significant impact on how citizens felt about the issues in these cases, the rulings did have an important effect on how citizens felt about the Court. The evidence Hoekstra uses comes from a series of two-wave panel studies conducted prior to and following the Supreme Court's decisions. This book provides important insights into how the public learns about Supreme Court decisions and how support for the Court is incrementally gained and lost as it announces its decisions.

Valerie J. Hoekstra is Assistant Professor of Political Science at Arizona State University. She was previously an Assistant Professor of Political Science and Fellow in the Center in Political Economy at Washington University in St. Louis. Hoekstra has published articles in *American Political Science Review*, *Journal of Politics*, and *American Politics Quarterly*.

Public Reaction to Supreme Court Decisions

VALERIE J. HOEKSTRA

Arizona State University

CAMBRIDGE
UNIVERSITY PRESS

PUBLISHED BY THE PRESS SYNDICATE OF THE UNIVERSITY OF CAMBRIDGE
The Pitt Building, Trumpington Street, Cambridge, United Kingdom

CAMBRIDGE UNIVERSITY PRESS
The Edinburgh Building, Cambridge CB2 2RU, UK
40 West 20th Street, New York, NY 10011-4211, USA
477 Williamstown Road, Port Melbourne, VIC 3207, Australia
Ruiz de Alarcón 13, 28014 Madrid, Spain
Dock House, The Waterfront, Cape Town 8001, South Africa

http://www.cambridge.org

First published 2003

Printed in the United States of America

Typeface Sabon 10/13 pt.   *System* LaTeX 2_ε [TB]

A catalog record for this book is available from the British Library.

Library of Congress Cataloging in Publication Data

Hoekstra, Valerie J., 1968–
Public reaction to Supreme Court decisions / Valerie J. Hoekstra.
   p.   cm.
Includes bibliographical references and index.
ISBN 0-521-82058-8 (hardback)
1. United States. Supreme Court – Public opinion.   2. Judgments – United States – Public
opinion.   3. Constitutional law – United States – Public opinion.   I. Title.
KF8748.H63   2003
347.73'26–dc21   2003040903

ISBN 0 521 82058 8 hardback

For Michael

Contents

Figures

Tables

Acknowledgments

Studying the effect of Supreme Court decisions on public opinion has proven to be a difficult task. There simply has not been a wealth of data out there to work with. This was the very issue I was grappling with until Jeffrey Segal stopped me in the hallway of the Political Science Department at Stony Brook. He told me there was a case from Long Island going to the Supreme Court and that I should think about "doing something with it." His suggestion served as the impetus for an earlier part of this research project, which we worked on together, and, ultimately, for this book. For this and for his continued advice and support, I am incredibly grateful. While Jeff's comment started me thinking about how to do something with that Long Island case, it was support from the National Science Foundation (NSF) and the departments of Political Science at SUNY Stony Brook and Washington University in St. Louis that made it possible to do so. At Stony Brook, I was given access to staff offices to call residents of Long Island. A grant from NSF (SBR 9423032) made it possible to pay for the long-distance calls and to train and pay interviewers to conduct many of the calls. I am also indebted to John Sprague, who, as chair of the Political Science Department at Washington University in St. Louis, set up a makeshift survey center so that I could continue to conduct interviews from St. Louis.

In addition, I have benefited from the wisdom of many others who have generously read and commented on different parts of the manuscript at one point or another. I hope I have faithfully incorporated their comments; but, of course, I take full responsibility for the flaws that remain. In particular I am indebted to Lawrence Baum, Gregory Caldeira, Brad Canon, Robert Durr, Lee Epstein, Stanley Feldman, Ada Finifter,

Charles Franklin, James Gibson, Brandon Haller, Clark Hubbard, Leonie Huddy, Renee Johnson, Bradford Jones, Liane Kosaki, Milton Lodge, Thomas Marshall, Kathleen McGraw, Gary Miller, Jeffrey Mondak, Richard Pacelle, Gerald Rosenberg, Jennifer Segal, Elliot Slotnick, and Stephen Wasby. I would also like to thank the numerous anonymous reviewers who have seen and commented on this research in different forms and on related projects.

I am further indebted to those who assisted in the data collection. I would have nothing to say without their help interviewing the hundreds of respondents who participated in this project. In particular, I wish to acknowledge the assistance of Scott Comparato, Paul Djupe, Andrew Dutlinger, Lauretta Frederking, Jill Glathar, Timothy Johnson, and Madhavi McCall. I would have even less to say without the willingness and graciousness of hundreds of people across the country to talk with complete strangers about their political beliefs and their personal situations without any tangible benefit to them. I did numerous interviews myself and can still vividly remember many of these people and their circumstances. I am grateful for their time and insights.

At Cambridge University Press, Lewis Bateman has been a wonderfully supportive and good-humored editor. He made the review process as painless as possible, offered helpful comments, and importantly, made the process as expeditious as possible, even when I did little to help him out on this. To this point, I am also incredibly grateful for the reviewers' considerable time and effort. Each of these reviewers, as well as the reviewers at Princeton University Press, made this a much better, more focused book. I sincerely thank each of them. I would also like to thank Chuck Myers at Princeton University Press who also helped transform this project into a book and went to great lengths on my behalf.

Finally, I am forever indebted to my family. My parents were, and continue to be, an important source of support in my life. Had it not been for the constant love, support, and prodding from my husband, Michael Nickelsburg, I simply would not have been able to finish this book. Without complaint, he gave me the luxury of time to finish even when it came at the expense of my other responsibilities. Beyond the infinite supply of emotional support and encouragement, he painstakingly read and reread chapters, and, in general, served as a sounding board for my (often half-baked) ideas and for my (mostly self-made) frustrations. Most important of all, I want to thank him because every day he made me want to work hard so that I could turn off the computer and focus on our wonderful life together and on our precious son, Samuel Emerson.

The High-Wire Act

The Supreme Court and Public Opinion

"The Court's authority – possessed of neither the purse nor the sword –
ultimately rests on sustained public confidence in its moral sanction."
– Justice Felix Frankfurter[1]

Every few decades, the Supreme Court hands down a monumental decision that grasps both public and elite attention. It is almost impossible to think of the Court without conjuring up images of such decisions as *Brown v. Board of Education* (1954), *Roe v. Wade* (1973), and most recently, *Bush v. Gore* (2000). Each was followed by intense media coverage, heated debate among citizens and scholars alike about the issues in the cases, as well as discussions about the very legitimacy of the Court itself.

After *Bush v. Gore*, for example, many people wondered whether the ultimate winner of this strange presidential election would have an effective mandate to govern. The question on every mind, and at the forefront of many discussions, was whether or not the Court's decision would be able to cast legitimacy on an otherwise disputable electoral outcome. After a majority on the Court ruled in support of George W. Bush in what appeared to be a closely divided partisan and ideological division, a new topic of discussion emerged. Now, in addition to discussions about whether the Court could cast legitimacy on Bush's presidential administration, speculation about the consequences of the decision for the Court itself quickly emerged. By entering into such a contentious and political dispute, would the Court's decision ultimately cause itself immediate and

[1] *Baker v. Carr* (1962).

long-term damage? In his dissent, Justice John Paul Stevens clearly thinks so. He writes

The endorsement of that position by the majority of this Court can only lend credence to the most cynical appraisal of the work of judges throughout the land. It is confidence in the men and women who administer the judicial system that is the true backbone of the rule of law. Time will one day heal the wound to that confidence that will be inflicted by today's decision. One thing, however, is certain. Although we may never know with complete certainty the identity of the winner of this year's Presidential election, the identity of the loser is perfectly clear. It is the Nation's confidence in the judge as an impartial guardian of the rule of law. I respectfully dissent.

While *Bush v. Gore* is the most recent and salient example, it is not unique by any means. The Court has found itself in other controversies of similar magnitude. In *Brown v. Board of Education*, for example, the Court found itself embroiled in one of the most important and entrenched political and legal battles of the twentieth century. Both before and after the Court announced its decision, people questioned whether the Court's decision would be implemented and whether the decision would promote advances in civil rights more generally. At the same time, the very divisiveness of the issue caused speculation about whether the Court's decision would affect support for the Court itself. What would be the implications for the Court if the decision was ignored, evaded, or outright defied? Could the Court's legitimacy withstand the possible aftermath? The repercussions of *Roe v. Wade* were similar. While the decision required less action from public officials (Rosenberg 1991), the Court's involvement in abortion generates a great deal of negative attention. These concerns about implementation and Court legitimacy seem inevitable following the announcement of such contentious, salient, and divisive issues.

What about the mundane decisions that make up the Court's docket each year? What effect can and do these ordinary decisions have on public opinion? After all, cases such as *Bush v. Gore*, *Roe v. Wade*, and *Brown v. Board of Education* are the exceptions, not the rule. In any given term, only one or two of the Court's decisions, if any, will generate significant national controversy and attention. Is there any public interest and attention to these other, more ordinary cases? Do these decisions have any effect on public opinion? Do these decisions factor into public support for the Court? These are the questions addressed in this book.

In cases such as *Brown v. Board of Education*, *Roe v. Wade*, and *Bush v. Gore*, the consequences are often enormous. But every case has consequences, even if those consequences are not felt nationally. Every case represents a conflict between two parties on an issue broad enough to merit our highest Court's attention. Every Supreme Court decision will affect some segment of the population and will attract some media attention. The question is whether these ordinary decisions representing the vast majority of the Court's work have any effect on public opinion or on support for the Court.

This book examines media coverage and public reaction to four Supreme Court decisions in the communities where the controversies began. The cases included are representative of ones the Court regularly considers each term. Not one generates the kind of attention paid to cases such as *Bush v. Gore, Brown v. Board of Education*, or *Roe v. Wade*. Still, as is true with most of the Court's cases, they were important and had consequences to the parties and to their communities. Thus, they may attract more intense and sustained local media interest, providing us with the opportunity to learn about the effect of these local cases among community members.

Looking to the effect in local communities is important for a number of reasons. First, if we assume that only the huge national landmark cases affect public opinion, in essence, we are saying that the remainder of the Court's work is inconsequential, at least in terms of public opinion. Moreover, examinations of national public opinion data may (falsely) confirm this. Using national data, it may be possible to connect cases such as *Bush v. Gore* to changes in public opinion and support for the Court (Kritzer 2001; Gibson, Caldeira, and Spence 2001). But at the national level, the effect of other, more routine decisions may look unsystematic and not clearly connected to public opinion or institutional support.

However, beneath the noise may actually be systematic effects – ones not easily detectable or the same for all citizens – but systematic nonetheless. If citizens learn about different Court decisions based on information available and salient to them, then looking for uniform national level effects is misguided. This does not mean that Court decisions are without national effect. If the Court's effect is more localized – either in terms of geography or some other process – we might still see the effect of Court decisions on public opinion and that Court decisions might affect support for the Court on a national level. The process is just more subtle and possibly more gradual. Another reason to look at local public opinion is that Court decisions frequently require active implementation, oftentimes by local officials. If the Court can change public opinion on the issues, or at least cast legitimacy on the policy under review, the probability of successful implementation is greatly enhanced (Canon and Johnson 1998). In short, a better understanding of the effects of Court decisions on local public opinion is important to a more complete understanding of the more general relationship between the Court and public opinion.

Included in the analysis is an examination of the quality and quantity of media coverage and subsequent levels of local awareness, the effect of those decisions on attitudes toward the issues in the cases, and finally, changes in support for the Court in the wake of these decisions. The unique data collected for this project come from four two-wave panel studies measuring citizens' attitudes prior to and following the Supreme Court's decisions in the local communities where the controversies began. Unlike most previous work on the Court and public opinion which relies on *static, national* samples and *aggregate-level* public opinion data, the panel data provide better insights into the dynamic process of opinion change, the effect in communities where access to information is sufficient to observe an effect, and finally, the effect at the individual level. The goal of this book is to help shed light on the nature of the relationship between the Supreme Court and public opinion by taking the logic of the experimental approach and implementing it in the context of a real-world situation.

THE SUPREME COURT AND PUBLIC OPINION

Although researchers have been interested in the relationship between the Court and public opinion for decades, and this research has produced a significant body of research, we do not really know the answers to many of the most pressing questions about the Supreme Court and public opinion. Unlike scholars of Congress or the presidency, scholars of the Court seem content to assume that the Court's decisions, besides the occasional *Roe v. Wade, Brown v. Board of Education,* or now *Bush v. Gore,* have little or no effect. In part, this assumption comes from national public opinion polls that show: 1) scant knowledge about the Court and its activities, 2) few aggregate shifts in support for issues on which the Court has decided, and 3) few aggregate shifts in support for the Court. But, these questions are about individual level behavior, and so they require research on individual level changes in response to actual Supreme Court decisions.

On the other hand, the question of whether public opinion affects Supreme Court decision making is hotly debated and systematically investigated in the profession's leading journals (Mishler and Sheehan 1993, 1996; Norpoth and Segal 1994; Stimson, MacKuen, and Erikson 1995; Flemming and Wood 1997). Although debate continues, some of this research concludes that public opinion has a direct effect on the justices' decisions (Mishler and Sheehan 1993, 1996; Stimson et al. 1995;

Flemming and Wood 1997). But, if the Court's support is insulated from public reactions to its decisions, as we have been content to assume, why should it care about whether its decisions reflect current preferences? The main reason is that implicit in this line of research is that Court decisions, contrary to public opinion, have negative consequences for the Court. Such decisions affect the Court's legitimacy or may lead to the lack of implementation or outright defiance of its mandates. It is difficult to reconcile the assumptions in this line of inquiry with the assumption that Court decisions have little to no effect on public opinion or support for the Court.

In some respects, comparisons with Congress or the presidency are neither appropriate nor fair. Unlike its democratically selected and accountable counterparts, the Supreme Court appears relatively isolated from and unconstrained by public opinion. Its members do not run for election, and once in office, they essentially serve for life. While this certainly places them in an enviable position, the justices must rely on public support for the implementation of their policies since they possess "neither the purse nor the sword." The Court's lack of many enforcement mechanisms makes public support even more essential to the Court than it is to other institutions. This public support may generate an important source of political capital for the Court (Choper 1980).

The political capital on which the Court relies when it hands down controversial decisions, according to many accounts, is its relatively high and stable levels of popularity among members of the mass public (Choper 1980; Mondak 1992, 1994; Hoekstra 1995; Mondak and Smithey 1997). Indeed, support for the Court is consistently higher than for either Congress or the president (Marshall 1989; Hibbing and Theiss-Morse 1995; Mondak and Smithey 1997). While many researchers believe the Court's popularity can influence public opinion, and such effects have been found in experimental tests, this relationship proves difficult to demonstrate outside the laboratory setting. Similarly difficult to uncover is the relationship between the Court's decisions and support for the institution. If the Court's level of support is a valuable commodity, it is important to understand whether its decisions ultimately affect its supply of this commodity. In other words, is the Court's support an *expendable* and *exhaustible* commodity?

Hypotheses

This section elaborates on the specific research hypotheses examined in the empirical chapters. The hypotheses are broadly divided into the following topics: 1) media coverage, public awareness, and perceptions of the importance of the issue in the Court's decision; 2) change in opinion on the issues contained in the case; and 3) change in support for the Court following its decisions.

Media Coverage and Public Knowledge

Although the research on the relationship between public opinion and the Supreme Court is rife with contradictions, it is possible to draw some preliminary conclusions. First, national public opinion polls typically report low levels of knowledge about the Supreme Court (Caldeira 1991). Most cases simply do not appear to resonate on the national agenda. However, reliance on national public opinion polls may be part of the problem. Simply stated, most Americans read their local paper, not *The New York Times*. If a story does not appear in the media to which most people are attuned, they simply will not have the opportunity to encounter any information about the Court. Instead, it is necessary to look to those places where access to information is sufficient to produce informed citizens.

Examples of this are found in existing research. For example, Berkson's (1978) examination of occupational groups found high levels of information regarding cases that had some bearing on job-related activities. Kritzer's (2001) analysis of the effect of *Bush v. Gore* shows that the extensive media coverage of that decision provided a bit of a civics lesson in that people learned other things about the Court as well. Franklin and his colleagues (Franklin, Kosaki, and Kritzer 1993; Franklin and Kosaki 1995) found high levels of attention in both a national and city (St. Louis) sample when they conducted their interviews shortly after the Court announced its decisions. This research clearly supports the conclusion that decisions about *where* and *when* to sample are important to consider.

Thus, one obvious place to look, the *where* part of the equation, is in the local communities where the controversies began. There, the local media should be more likely to report on a local case that makes it to the Supreme Court than on a similar case that originates in some other part of the country (Graber 1997). If the media do report about these cases, then it is reasonable to expect local levels of awareness to be high. While research suggests that the media may not be able to change how people think about issues, it can certainly tell them which issues are important to think about (Iyengar and Kinder 1987; Iyengar 1991). This leads to the following two hypotheses:

Media Coverage Hypothesis: The local media should cover local cases more extensively than the national media and media from other parts of the nation.

Local/National Awareness Hypothesis: Because of the local saturation of media coverage, levels of awareness in these local communities will be higher than typically found in national samples.

While local media coverage is expected to be high, producing highly informed citizens throughout the local communities, those from the *immediate* communities should have even more interest in these cases than will their neighbors in the surrounding communities. The work by Franklin and Kosaki (1995) suggests that while media coverage is critical, it is only one important predictor of knowledge of Supreme Court decisions. Individual citizens bring their own interests, biases, and abilities to the table as well. Those who are more engaged in politics, are better educated, and have a greater interest in an issue, for example, are more likely to learn about a Supreme Court case even when information is relatively high. For instance, Catholics should be more attuned to cases affecting abortion rights, and African Americans to cases about desegregation or affirmative action, even though the general public has equal access to information about the cases.

Since the conflict started in the *immediate* community – often involving local public officials, local issues, local groups, and even neighbors – all else equal, the residents of the immediate communities will actively seek out and pay greater attention to information than will their counterparts in the surrounding communities, even where *access* to the information is equal. This leads to the second awareness hypothesis:

Immediate/Surrounding Awareness Hypothesis: Levels of awareness among residents in the immediate communities will be higher than among residents of the surrounding communities.

Local Perceptions of Importance

Implicit in this hypothesis is that residents of the local community should feel more strongly about the issue and perceive it to be more important than do the residents of the surrounding communities. Why would the local residents care about this issue more than would those from the surrounding communities? One of the cases pits members of the logging industry in Oregon against the northern spotted owl. In that community, Sweet Home, Oregon, the economic well-being of the community was greatly affected by the Court's decision. So, at least in this case, material self-interest was directly implicated. This is one straightforward route to policy importance. For this reason alone, one would expect the residents of this logging community to attach greater policy relevance to the Supreme Court case than those from the surrounding communities. But there are other routes to policy relevance.

In the following three cases, there was little or no direct connection with material self-interest. At issue in another case was whether the state of Oklahoma could collect taxes on gasoline sold by Native Americans. While clearly this case involves an economic issue, there were only two filling stations owned by members of the tribe challenging the tax. So, it is unlikely that many other non-Native Americans who owned filling stations were really in economic competition with the Native American stations. Another case involves a school board's denial of a request by a local church pastor to show a religiously inspired film in the high school auditorium. In yet another case, the issue was whether a state legislature could create a special school district for disabled Hasidic school children whose parents did not want them to have to interact with non-Hasidic children. In these last three cases, clearly, the issue was not material self-interest.

So, why might the local residents be more interested in these cases and feel more strongly about the issues? They should care for the simple reason that perceptions of importance do not need to derive from the implication of some tangible material self-interest. In fact, social psychologists emphasize the *subjective* sense of importance (Boninger, Krosnick, and Berent 1995). Another source of the perception of importance can include such considerations as identifying with the people involved (e.g., members of groups in the local community) (Krosnick, Boninger, and Chuang 1993; Boninger, et al. 1995). So, when a Court case involves individuals or groups from one's own community, it is reasonable to expect that individual to feel more strongly about the issue than if the exact same case originated in some other town or community. If it is happening elsewhere to other people, it is just not as compelling. Thus, residents of the immediate communities should feel more strongly about the issues in a Supreme Court case than those from the surrounding communities. This leads to the fourth hypothesis:

Local Importance Hypothesis: Those from the immediate community should perceive the case as more important than those from the surrounding communities.

Can Court Decisions Shape Public Opinion?

Many scholars believe that the Court can sway people in the direction of its decisions. This belief dates back to Dahl's work on the legitimacy conferring capacity of the Court (1957). According to Dahl, the Supreme Court is rarely out of step with lawmaking majorities. Instead, the Court lends legitimacy to the policies of the other branches of government. Implicit in this statement is that the Court *can* lend its legitimacy to these policies. Since Dahl's seminal work, scholars have attempted to test this implication – with mixed success.

In one of the most exhaustive studies of the effect of Court decisions on public opinion, Marshall (1988, 1989) found that following Supreme Court decisions, there is very little evidence of aggregate opinion shifts in the direction of the decisions. Similarly, Rosenberg (1991) argues those Court decisions, specifically *Roe v. Wade* and *Brown v. Board of Education*, did very little on their own to change policy, access to abortion, or public attitudes on race. By no means has Rosenberg's analysis been the final word, however. In particular, Canon and Johnson (1998) argue that on many policy issues in the twentieth century, the Court has been effective in bringing about social change, even in the face of opposition from other political actors.

In contrast to the "null effects" literature, Franklin and Kosaki's (1989) research on abortion attitudes in the wake of *Roe v. Wade*, and Johnson and Martin's (1998) research on capital punishment, emphasized the need to look beyond persuasion as the only structure of response to Court decisions. Franklin and Kosaki (1989) found that on the less controversial dimensions of abortion policy (abortion in the case of rape, incest, or to preserve the woman's health) the Court's decision increased public support. But on the more controversial issue of discretionary abortions, they found that Court decisions actually polarized public opinion. In other words, those who initially supported discretionary abortion became more supportive; those who previously opposed, became increasingly opposed. Johnson and Martin (1998) found similar results in their examination of public response to Court decisions on capital punishment. Both groups of authors suspect that polarization is limited to such visible and controversial issues, and that this structure of opinion change may not be the same pattern observed for other kinds of cases. Less controversial issues, such as the ones included in this book, may be where persuasion is more likely to occur. Such a hypothesis is further buttressed by the findings of experimental research that found that Court decisions can positively influence public opinion (Mondak 1990, 1991, 1992, 1994; Hoekstra 1995; but see Bass and Thomas 1984).[2]

---

[2] The section on research design discusses one possible explanation for why it is that experimental research has been so much more successful in detecting persuasion than have

Given these previous findings, what kind of effect of Court decisions on public opinion might we expect? Three possibilities emerge from the earlier discussion: persuasion, no effect, or polarization. Polarization was found following highly salient and controversial decisions dealing with abortion and capital punishment, and is less likely to occur following the more routine kinds of cases the Court hears each term. The null findings are based largely on aggregate data which can obscure individual level effects. With individual level data, more subtle patterns might emerge. Finally, persuasion has been found, mostly in the experimental studies where attitudes are measured soon after exposure to information about a Court decision and where the measures are created with specific issues in mind. Therefore, even though the results from past research appear somewhat contradictory, by examining *individual* level opinion, and following more *routine* cases where media, and hence, public attention is high, persuasion effects are quite possible.

But persuasion is a complicated process and it may not occur for all people in equal measures. To understand the conditions where persuasion is most likely to result, it is first necessary to understand more about the processes underlying persuasion.

Research from social psychology provides guidance. In short, this research shows that persuasion varies with individual and situational factors (Petty and Cacioppo 1986).[3] First, for persuasion to occur, individuals must hear and think about a persuasive message, such as a Court decision. However, simple knowledge of a Court decision does not necessarily lead to persuasion – the process is slightly more complicated.

At one end of the spectrum, some individuals hear the information, but do not spend a great deal of time thinking about the issue. At the other end, there are individuals with prior information or who feel strongly about the issue and are motivated to think about and process information about the issue, but they also "have greater ability to do so. Thus, when a message contains information that is inconsistent with subjects' initial opinions, high relevance subjects should be more motivated and generally more able to generate counterarguments to the arguments presented" (Petty and Cacioppo 1986, 146; see also Fiske and Taylor 1991, 205–52). In other words, the more important the issue is to an individual, the greater

traditional survey-based approaches. In short, some argue that the positive findings of experimental research are simply artifacts of the research approach. For example, some argue that experiments artificially increase knowledge of decisions among people least likely to learn about the decisions outside of the experimental lab.

[3] The following discussion is adopted from Hoekstra and Segal (1996).

the motivation to pay attention to, and spend time thinking about, the issue and its political implications (Petty and Cacioppo 1986; Fiske and Taylor 1992; Krosnick et al. 1993). This expectation is also supported by recent research on the role of certain affective responses on political evaluations. In their work on candidate evaluation, Marcus and MacKuen (1993) observed that heightened anxiety about personally relevant issues should increase attention to political information (see also Wyer et al. 1991).

Since those in the immediate community are expected to perceive the issue as more important (*The Importance Hypothesis*), their opinions should be more difficult to change. They are more likely to seek out and critically think about the different information. This thinking, or message elaboration, should mediate the impact of the Court's persuasive appeal. Overall, these people should be less likely to change their opinion on the issue in the direction of the Court's decision. Those from the surrounding communities, however, might become more supportive of the Court's decision. They too should be exposed to sufficient information, but they are expected to care somewhat less strongly about this issue than their counterparts in the immediate community, and thus spend less time thinking about the different dimensions to the issue. This leads to the first opinion change hypothesis:

Opinion Change/Town of Residence Hypothesis: *All else equal, those from the surrounding communities will change their opinion in the direction of the Court's decision more than those from the immediate community.*

The final consideration is the role of source characteristics. In order to increase the persuasive appeal of a message, individuals must be positively disposed toward the source of the message. One of the most central findings in the persuasion literature is that source credibility is critical (Petty and Cacioppo 1986; Fiske and Taylor 1992). Moreover, experimental research on the Supreme Court's persuasive ability emphasizes the role of support for the Court (Mondak 1990, 1991, 1992, 1994; Hoekstra 1995). Thus, those who start off with higher levels of support ought to be more likely to change their opinion in the direction of the Court's decision. Those who hold a less generous opinion of the Court should be less influenced by the Court's decision. This leads to the second of the opinion change hypotheses:

Opinion Change/Support for Court Hypothesis: *Those with initially higher levels of support for the Court should show greater change in the direction of the Court's decision than those with lower levels of support for the Court.*

Finally, the effect of support for the Court on attitude change should be contingent upon town of residence. Specifically, the effect of support for the Court (i.e., source credibility) should be strongest among those from the surrounding communities (those with less strongly held opinions) than those from the immediate community. This leads to the third and final opinion change hypothesis:

Town of Residence/Court Support Interaction Hypothesis: The effect of support for the Court on opinion change should be conditioned on respondents' town of residence.

Sources of Support for the Court

Most accounts of public support for the Supreme Court refer to the Court's legitimacy as an institution of government. Much of the recent research focuses on two particular concepts: diffuse and specific support. Diffuse support for the Court refers to relatively enduring attitudes about the role of the Court in our constitutional scheme of government. Specific support, on the other hand, refers more to evaluations of the Court's actions (Caldeira 1986; Caldeira and Gibson 1992; see also Jaros and Roper 1980; Murphy and Tanenhaus 1968a, 1968b, 1972, 1981). To many, these sources of support should be distinct; and, the prevailing consensus is that they are, especially among members of the mass public (Caldeira and Gibson 1992). Scholars who are interested in questions about specific and diffuse support typically are interested in different questions from the ones posed in this project. Often, the aim of that research is to understand the sources of diffuse support for the institution, and thus they wish to remove the influence of support for specific decisions from measures of diffuse support.

But, the bottom line is that most of this research suggests that agreement with specific Court decisions does not typically factor into overall support for the institution. Even so, this research does not preclude the impact of decisions. Rather, it assumes some dynamic component to the process, where especially notable or activist decisions may factor into the equation (Caldeira and Gibson 1992). Also, Mondak and Smithey's (1997) research suggests that while individual attitudes toward the Court are generally positive, these attitudes may change as a result of controversial and unpopular decisions. The main implication is that the high and stable aggregate levels of support for the Court do not preclude individual variability in response to Court decisions.

Research by Grosskopf and Mondak (1998) and Kritzer (2001) establishes a strong empirical link between actual decisions and support for the Supreme Court. Grosskopf and Mondak examined the effect of two controversial decisions on support for the Court (*Webster v. Reproductive Health Services* and *Texas v. Johnson*) and showed that support for these decisions affected support for the Court. In fact, they found that disagreement outweighs agreement. Kritzer (2001) reported systematic partisan shifts in support for the Court among partisan groups in the wake of *Bush v. Gore*. Thus, there is good reason to suspect that support for specific decisions affects overall support for the institution.

Other research focuses on the Court's procedures, such as the secrecy of deliberations, infrequent media attention, and perceptions of being removed from partisan political battles both within the Court and between the Court and other branches of government. All this leads to high levels of public confidence in the Court compared with other institutions (Hibbing and Theiss-Morse 1995). Indeed, aggregate levels of support for the Court are consistently higher than levels of support for Congress and the executive, and they appear relatively more stable as well (Marshall 1989; Hibbing and Theiss-Morse 1995; Mondak and Smithey 1997). Though the data on aggregate public support for the Court are consistent with this process argument, the data are also consistent with citizens hearing about certain Supreme Court cases and changing their perception of the Court in response. As Mondak and Smithey note, "Individual level change does not necessarily preclude aggregate level stability" (1997, 1139).

The process argument bases its findings largely on aggregate measures of support for all three national institutions with little attention paid to variation at the individual level. Like the other explanations of support for the Court, the process argument does not entirely preclude the possibility for Court decisions to factor into evaluations of the Court. Rather, Hibbing and Theiss-Morse (1995) simply note that the role of process has been underappreciated in research on Congress. So, while scholarly accounts may underestimate the role of process in support for Congress, it is just the opposite in the study of public support for the Court. It seems as though our attention to process arguments has come at the expense of policy arguments.

Do Court decisions affect public support for the Court? If they do, the most straightforward effect would be that evaluations should change according to how the individual initially felt about the issue. All else equal, those who initially agree with the position the Court ultimately takes should become increasingly supportive of the Court following the decision. Those who disagree should become less supportive. This leads to the first hypothesis about how support for the Court should change in response to the Court's decision.

Change in Support for the Court Hypothesis: Those who initially agree (disagree) with the Court's ultimate position should show an increase (decrease) in support for the Court.

Finally, while there are no hypotheses about how town of residence, on its own, affects change in support for the Court, town of residence is expected to interact with prior opinion on the issue in a way similar to the interactive effect described in the previous section on opinion change. In particular, since those in the immediate community are expected to rate the issue as more important, and have more strongly held opinions, they will also attach greater weight to (dis)agreement with the Court's decision than those from the surrounding communities. This leads to the final hypothesis:

Town of Residence/Support for the Court Hypothesis: The effect of policy agreement on support for the Court should be conditioned on town of residence. Those from the immediate community should attach greater significance to the decision, and thus show greater change according to how they initially felt about the issue.

RESEARCH DESIGN

The following pages briefly describe the research strategy and data collection. More detailed descriptions can be found in the Appendices. This discussion explains why these important questions about the Court and public opinion remain largely unanswered. Many of us suspect that Court decisions must have some impact on public opinion. Likewise, some of us suspect that its decisions are, at least in part, connected with public support for the institution. Unfortunately, there is only scant empirical evidence to support our suspicions, and as the following discussion shows, the evidence that does exist is often contradictory.

The Standard Approaches to the Study of the Supreme Court and Public Opinion

The most common techniques used to study the Court and public opinion are static cross-sectional survey research, longitudinal cross sections, and laboratory experiments. Each of these approaches has advantages and can illuminate some questions about the relationship between the Court and public opinion. However, each also has limitations, at least for answering the questions central to this book. The list of shortcomings includes the following: 1) the failure to incorporate the dynamic nature of the process, 2) the failure to incorporate measures that closely reflect the subtlety of the issues involved in actual Court cases, 3) the failure to be able to generalize beyond the confines of the laboratory, and finally 4) the failure to identify appropriate populations from which to sample (Caldeira 1991; Hoekstra and Segal 1996).[4]

In order to facilitate the review of approaches incorporated in previous research, Table 1-1 presents a summary of relevant research on the Court and public opinion. The table organizes the research according to research design and data, categorizing each study as falling into one of four broad approaches: 1) static cross-sectional, 2) longitudinal (including longitudinal cross-sectional, non-panel quasi-experiments, time series of aggregate public opinion, and time series of aggregate indicators of policy change), 3) experimental data, and 4) panel studies. The table also includes the main research question of each of the entries. Projects that ask multiple questions contain multiple entries. Also, since a few of these studies include questions that are not directly relevant to this project, the table entries are restricted to the research questions that are most directly related. The third column briefly describes the research design and data source for each of these projects. The fourth column summarizes the relevant results.

Static Cross-Sectional Approaches

Of the three basic approaches – static, longitudinal, or experimental – the static cross section is probably the least suited to studying the *dynamic* effect of Court decisions on public opinion. But, as Table 1-1 reveals, it is the single most common approach to the study of the Supreme Court and public opinion. Static, or one-shot cross sections, can provide us with very useful information, such as how individual characteristics (e.g., ideology, education, commitment to democratic values, and engagement in political affairs) are related to knowledge about and support for the Court (Gibson 1989; Franklin and Kosaki 1995; Caldeira

---

[4] This laundry list of flaws is something that scholars of the Court have long recognized. In the same review mentioned previously, Caldeira (1991) noted that one of the hindrances to a full understanding of many issues related to the Court and public opinion is that scholars of the Court have had relatively poor data with which to work.

TABLE 1-1. *Previous Research: Question, Design, and Results*

Author	Specific Research Question	Research Design/Data	Results
		Static Cross-Sectional Data	
Kessel (1966)	Support for the Supreme Court.	A cross-sectional sample from Seattle, Washington (respondents were reminded of issues in recent cases).	Respondents were generally supportive of Court. Pro-Court messages reinforce support for the Court.
Dolbeare (1967)	Support for the Supreme Court.	A cross-sectional sample from Wisconsin.	Court benefits from low levels of attention. Support related to partisanship.
Murphy and Tanenhaus (1968a)	1) Knowledge of Court decisions.	A national cross section after the 1964 presidential election.	Approximately 41% claimed to pay attention. Of these, 60% could name a specific like/dislike (mostly civil rights and school prayer).
	2) Effect of Goldwater criticism on support for Court.	Same	Support for Court related to support for civil rights.
Murphy and Tanenhaus (1968b)	1) Knowledge of specific decisions.	National cross sections after 1964 and 1966 elections.	Approximately 40–45% could name a Court decision they liked or disliked.
	2) Specific/Diffuse support for the Court.	Same	Some evidence that recall of decisions related to support. Ideology also a predictor of support for the Court.

16

Adamany (1973)	Effect of Court decisions on public opinion.	A cross-sectional survey.	No effect.
Casey (1974)	Determinants of support for Court.	State-wide cross-sectional survey (Missouri).	Ideology is a strong predictor of support for the Court.
Berkson (1978)	Awareness of Court decisions among relevant occupational groups.	Surveys of different occupational groups.	High levels of knowledge of job-relevant cases.
Sigelman (1979)	Differences in black/white support for the Supreme Court.	National public opinion data over various years (1973–1977), aggregated into one cross section.	Any previous differences in levels of support disappears in 1970s.
Handberg and Maddox (1982)	Support for the Supreme Court.	National cross-sectional public opinion data.	Race and education explain support for the Court.
Adamany and Grossman (1983)	1) Knowledge of Supreme Court decisions.	Cross-sectional survey of the residents of Wisconsin.	Majority of respondents (62.3%) could not name a decision they either liked or disliked.
	2) Support for the Supreme Court among politically active and inactive.	Various national cross-sectional surveys between 1964 and 1976.	Support strongest among liberal activists.
Gibson and Caldeira (1992)	Diffuse support for the Supreme Court among blacks.	Cross-sectional survey data with an oversample of blacks.	Diffuse support among blacks somewhat lower than in previous accounts, and somewhat lower than among whites. Some connection between previous Court decisions supportive of racial equality and lingering support for the Court.

(*continued*)

17

TABLE 1-1 (*continued*)

Author	Specific Research Question	Research Design/Data	Results
Caldeira and Gibson (1992)	Diffuse support for the Supreme Court.	Cross-sectional survey data.	Mass support for the Supreme Court is strongly related to political values (e.g., democracy and social order) as well as education, attentiveness, political efficacy, and ideology.
Franklin, Kosaki, and Kritzer (1993)	National levels of knowledge of Supreme Court decisions.	National random sample following announcement of Court decisions.	Relatively high levels of information. Awareness ranges from 0 to 40%.
Franklin and Kosaki (1995)	Public knowledge and support for the Court.	Random sample of St. Louis, Missouri shortly after conclusion of the Court's 1988/89 term.	Frequency of media coverage increases probability of awareness as do individual characteristics. Stronger correlation between ideology and support among the more knowledgeable respondents.
Gibson, Caldeira, and Baird (1998)	Legitimacy of High Courts.	National public opinion data on support for 18 high courts.	Diffuse support for high courts (including the Supreme Court) insulates courts from dissatisfaction with decisions.
Gibson, Caldeira, and Spence (2002)	1) The effect of *Bush v. Gore* on the legitimacy of the Supreme Court.	National cross-sectional data.	Some effect of support for the decision on support for the Court.

Longitudinal Data: Public Opinion Cross Sections and Other Time-Series Indicators

	2) The effect of the Court's legitimacy on support for *Bush v. Gore*.	Same	Institutional legitimacy had an effect on perceptions of the decision.
Dolbeare and Hammond (1968)	1) Knowledge of Court decisions.	A mix of state cross-sectional data (Wisconsin) and longitudinal cross sections.	Relatively low levels of knowledge in the state data.
	2) Support for the Court.	Same	Party identification and some support for a connection between support for decisions and support for the Court.
Caldeira (1986)	Aggregate Support for the Court.	Time-series data on support for the Court (1966–1984).	Aggregate support for the Court varies as a function of both political events (i.e., Watergate, presidential popularity) as well as judicial actions.
Marshall (1988, 1989)	1) Aggregate change in public opinion on issues related to Court decisions.	Aggregate shifts in public opinion from various public opinion polls.	Little or no effect.
	2) Aggregate support for Supreme Court.	Aggregate levels of support for Court relative to Congress and president.	Support for Court is consistently higher than support for Congress.
Franklin and Kosaki (1989)	Group-level shifts in public opinion toward abortion policy pre- and post-*Roe*.	Aggregate, group-level shifts derived from cross-sectional data.	Positive change on nondiscretionary abortion, but polarization of opinion on discretionary abortion.

(*continued*)

TABLE 1-1 (*continued*)

Author	Specific Research Question	Research Design/Data	Results
Rosenberg (1991)	Effect of Supreme Court decisions on social change.	Relies on multiple indicators of change: public opinion, policy, media coverage, etc.	Change attributed to other actors, not the Supreme Court.
Hibbing and Theiss-Morse (1995)	Explaining aggregate differences in levels of support for Congress and the Court.	Longitudinal data comparing support for national institutions.	Congress is less popular than Supreme Court because of the way Congress does its work.
Mondak and Smithey (1997)	Changes in aggregate support for the Supreme Court over time.	Time-series data on support for the Court (1972–1994).	Aggregate stability in support for the Court often belies individual-level change.
Grosskopf and Mondak (1998)	Effect of two visible Court decisions on Support for the Court.	Three national cross sections.	Specific support for these salient decisions affected support for the Court. Negative effects also reported.
Johnson and Martin (1998)	Change in support for capital punishment.	Aggregate, group-level shifts derived from cross-sectional data (similar to Franklin and Kosaki [1989]).	Polarization after initial decision, no change following subsequent decisions.
Durr, Martin, and Wolbrecht (2000)	Support for the Supreme Court.	Aggregate time-series analysis.	Support for the Court is a function of the degree of divergence between Court and public liberalism.
Kritzer (2001)	1) Effect of *Bush v. Gore* on support for the Court.	Repeated national cross sections.	No net impact, yet there were measurable shifts in support by partisanship.
	2) Effect of *Bush v. Gore* on knowledge of the Court.	Same	Increase in knowledge of the Court.

Experimental Data

Study	Topic	Method	Findings
Jaros and Roper (1980)	How "myth," specific support, and diffuse support affect legitimacy of decisions.	Experiment, but no control group.	None of the independent variables contribute to the likelihood of compliance.
Bass and Thomas (1984)	Effect of Supreme Court on policy support.	Experiment.	No change.
Gibson (1989)	Institutional legitimacy, procedural justice, and compliance.	Split-ballot experiment within a cross-sectional survey.	Supreme Court can increase compliance. Perceptions of procedural justice relatively ineffective.
Mondak (1990, 1994)	Effect of Supreme Court on policy support/legitimation.	Experiment.	Positive change.
Mondak (1991)	Effect of Supreme Court on institutional support.	Experiment.	Support for the Court related to content of its decisions.
Mondak (1992)	1) Effect of Supreme Court on policy support.	Experiment.	Positive change.
	2) Effect of unpopular Supreme Court decisions on institutional legitimacy.	Experiment.	Unpopular decisions can decrease Court's legitimacy.
Hoekstra (1995)	Effect of Supreme Court on policy support.	Experiment.	Positive change on some issues.
Segal (1995)	Diffuse/Specific support for the Supreme Court.	Experiment.	Some evidence that Court decisions affect support.

Panel Data

Study	Topic	Method	Findings
Tanenhaus and Murphy (1981)	Determinants of, and changes in support for the Court.	Two-wave panel study (1975 re-interviews of respondents from previous studies).	Changes unrelated to partisanship. Specific support for Court decisions is related to support.

and Gibson 1992; Gibson and Caldeira 1992), or toward issues it decides (e.g., abortion, affirmative action, prayer in school). Moreover, recent comparative work (Caldeira, Gibson, and Baird 1998) suggests the possibility of gaining leverage on more dynamic questions by comparing across high courts from different nations. Even so, static approaches often fail to tell us about the *dynamics* of how Court actions influence attitudes toward the Court or toward the issues it decides.

These static cross sections may also shed light on how much, if anything, people are able to recall about the Court's activities, which is similar to two of the hypotheses (*Local/National Awareness Hypothesis* and the *Immediate/Surrounding Awareness Hypothesis*). Asking people what they recall about the Court does not necessarily require a dynamic research design. Even so, a poll taken around the timing of national elections, rather than around the Court's calendar, is likely to underestimate public attention since most of its decisions are handed down at the end of the term. This fact is well illustrated by Franklin and his colleagues (Franklin, et al. 1993; Franklin and Kosaki 1995), who found relatively widespread knowledge of specific Court decisions immediately following those decisions. Their findings stand in stark contrast to previous research, which relied extensively on data collected around the timing of national elections (e.g., Murphy and Tanenhaus 1968a, 1968b; Tanenhaus and Murphy 1981) that reveals much lower levels of attention.[5] Besides poor timing, most of the cross sections are *national* cross sections. As discussed more explicitly later in Chapter 3, looking to national samples is likely to produce inappropriate and misleading results. Only the occasional and exceptional case receives significant and sustained media coverage nationally. Instead, coverage is generally more regional and localized.

As the final column of Table 1-1 shows, there is no clear pattern for the effect of Court decisions on public opinion. First, the awareness studies report very different results, with some revealing high levels of attention (Berkson 1978; Franklin, et al. 1993; Franklin and Kosaki 1995)

---

[5] Actually, the reported figures from both Franklin and his colleagues (1993, 1995) and Murphy and Tanenhaus (1968a, 1968b) appear similar. Both report awareness around 40 percent. But the measures of awareness are not comparable. Murphy and Tanenhaus rely on data collected by the Survey Research Center at the University of Michigan that asked respondents whether they could name a Court decision – *any* Court decision – they either liked or disliked. On the other hand, Franklin and his colleagues asked about knowledge of a *specific* Court decision. Therefore, one interpretation of their research is that it reveals much higher levels of awareness since it presents a more difficult task to recall such specific information.

while others are less optimistic (Murphy and Tanenhaus 1968a, 1968b; Adamany and Grossman 1983). As for whether Court decisions affect public opinion, there is even less evidence – consistent or otherwise – since this question has not been emphasized much in the research. On the other hand, there has been considerable attention to support for the Supreme Court using cross-sectional approaches. Very little of this research has been interested in or been able to establish a link between specific Court decisions and support for the Supreme Court.

Longitudinal Cross-Sectional Approaches

As the previous discussion suggests, a longitudinal approach is necessary, but not always a sufficient approach to studying the Court's effect on public opinion. The second section of Table 1-1 includes examples of research relying on repeated cross-sections, aggregate policy indicators, and aggregate time-series of public opinion. What each of these studies has in common is the explicit incorporation of time, and thus information on dynamic processes. Each also has in common the fact that the unit of analysis is not the individual – each is aggregated at some level.

The explicit incorporation of this longitudinal approach helps provide a better understanding of the relationship between the Court and public opinion. Although these studies include an overtime approach, many, but not all of them, fall short of the mark. The reasons include poor timing – they are not timed to reflect the Court's calendar, poor measurement – using measures not appropriate to the underlying goals of the project, and/or poor sampling – they do not identify and isolate the proper populations of citizens.

Frequently these studies look at public opinion at two separate points in time on issues related to Court cases, but they rely on two independent cross sections. Such an approach can examine how characteristics such as ideology, party identification, religion, and so forth, influence susceptibility to attitude change, but only by looking at *aggregates,* not *individuals.* Franklin and Kosaki (1989) devised a clever strategy to deal with this problem. Even though they had to rely on repeated cross-sectional data, they used individual characteristics to identify groups they expected to become either more or less supportive of abortion policy following *Roe v. Wade.* They discovered that those who were initially supportive of access to discretionary abortion became more supportive following *Roe,* while those who were initially opposed, specifically Catholics, became less supportive. By identifying groups based on individual level theory, they were able to avoid the typical problem that plagues cross-sectional data: the aggregation problem. Other research that simply looked at aggregate opinion pre- and post-*Roe v. Wade* would incorrectly show no effects (Marshall 1988, 1989). Johnson and Martin (1998) used the same approach and found similar results for the Court's capital punishment decisions. Grosskopf and Mondak (1998) also overcame the aggregation problem in their examination of the effect of two Court decisions (*Webster v. Reproductive Health Services* and *Texas v. Johnson*) on changes in support for the Court. So, while clever research strategies can often overcome some of the shortcomings presented by less than ideal data, whenever possible, *individual* level longitudinal data should still be the objective.

Some of the usual sources for public opinion data also include individual level panel data. The most obvious source is, again, the NES. Though these panel studies yield useful information on the dynamics of an election campaign, unfortunately they too suffer from flaws that make them less than valuable for scholars of the Court. The usual suspects plague this data too – poor measurement and poor timing. It is common to find measures of support for abortion, capital punishment, and even flag burning on the typical national public opinion survey. Yet it is next to impossible to find measures about support for specially created school districts, sovereignty of Native American tribes, equal access for religious groups to public facilities, government involvement in protecting endangered species, or various other issues at the center of most Court decisions. Thus, we can only speculate about public reaction to these more typical kinds of cases.

Experimental Approaches

The third approach is the use of an experimental design. Table 1-1 includes a list of some of the recent experiments investigating the relationship between the Supreme Court and public opinion. Experiments provide us with a wealth of insight into the relationship between the Court and public opinion, including interesting hypotheses that we can test outside of the lab. For example, some research suggests that the impact of Court decisions might vary by the issue in the case, how subjects feel about the issue initially, and how they feel about the Court initially (Mondak 1991, 1994; Hoekstra 1995; Segal 1995).

Experiments have an additional advantage: they often avoid obstacles present in many mass survey-based approaches. For example, they usually incorporate pre- and post-tests, thereby explicitly capturing the dynamics of change. Also, the measures are written specifically for understanding opinions on issues closely related to those issues in a Court decision. Finally, experiments are able to isolate the impact of the Court relative to other possible sources of influence. Experiments minimize the "noise" of the outside world to such an extent that we can confidently attribute the source of the influence to the Court. In other words, experiments can carefully and systematically avoid the pitfalls inherent in survey-based approaches; but, by doing so they may also lose the advantages inherent in surveys.

However, experiments have their own set of shortcomings. The main criticism of experimental approaches is the artificial nature of the setting. Such studies are typically conducted in a laboratory, usually involving college students who read about a hypothetical Supreme Court decision. This can be problematic when at least some of the reasons why people hear about Court decisions outside of the laboratory (such as political engagement, knowledge, or level of education) are related to whether attitudes toward the Court and/or policy issues are susceptible to change. Those with higher levels of education or who are more knowledgeable and involved in politics typically have opinions derived from greater stores of information and have greater confidence in their opinions. For these reasons, they are simply less susceptible to persuasion. If in the "real" world only the most educated or politically engaged citizens hear about Court decisions, but in the laboratory, *everyone* hears about the decisions, then the conclusions about the impact of decisions on political beliefs will likely be very different. The frequent use of college students as the subjects for these experiments compounds this problem. College students provide a curious mix of well-educated but also, arguably, fairly malleable individuals (Sears 1986). Education tends to solidify and inform our beliefs, decreasing the susceptibility to persuasion, and yet, these young subjects may not yet have firmly held attitudes. It is unclear how and whether this provides serious consequences for the research.[6]

These shortcomings aside, experiments have provided us with some of the most consistent results to date – results that provide continued support for the hypothesis that Court decisions might affect public opinion and support for the Court itself. As Table 1-1 reveals, experiments have consistently found that Court decisions can, under certain conditions,

---

[6] Experimental research has been an important tool to those who study the Supreme Court and public opinion. The critique applies only to the questions posed in this particular project.

affect support for the position taken by the Court and produce changes in support for the Court.

While many of the standard approaches to studying the relationship between the Court and public opinion have advantages, none addresses all three of the related issues central to this project: awareness of the decision, attitudes toward the issues in the cases, and attitudes toward the Court. Instead, it is necessary to find an approach that can capture how people learn about Court decisions in the real world, and at the same time capture how opinions and attitudes change in response to this learning process. As such, the design should be longitudinal. More than that, the subjects should be the same people before and after a Court decision, not two separate cross sections. Those sampled should come from populations that have some access to information about the decision. Finally, there should be increased attention to developing measures that capture the subtlety of the issues contained in Court decisions.

Panel Studies of Quasi-Experiments

The best way to accomplish this is to take the logic of the experimental approach, while allowing the Court itself to provide the experimental manipulation. Others have argued the benefits of such an approach. Caldeira (1991) suggested that panel studies of quasi-experiments might prove a fruitful avenue of research. Indeed, even before Caldeira's suggestion, some of the pioneers of the study of the Court and public opinion, Walter Murphy and Joseph Tanenhaus (1981) exploited panel data to examine some of the same questions advanced in this book (see Table 1-1).

While it approaches the ideal, their research had its limitations. First, the initial data were collected around the timing of national elections, not the Court's calendar, and thus might underestimate actual knowledge of Supreme Court decisions. Second, the research was not about the effect of specific Court decisions, but rather it asked respondents whether they could name anything the Court had done that they either liked or disliked. In other words, while it was indeed a true panel study, there was no real or single quasi-experimental manipulation. Third, and related, the ten-year gap precludes pinpointing the effect of specific decisions. Since the Court had decided hundreds of cases over this ten-year period, and had undergone significant compositional changes, it is virtually impossible to determine whether we can attribute change in support for the Court to anything specific the Court had done. Fourth, they rely on a national sample of respondents, and as demonstrated in Chapter 3, information about the Court may vary in different regions. Finally, while they are interested in some of the same questions (i.e., knowledge of Court decisions, how specific support affects diffuse support), they do not address one of the main questions: changes in support for the specific policies contained in Court decisions.

Despite previous shortcomings, panel studies are still the best approach for studying the questions in this book. Such an approach allows for assessing the real-world effects captured by standard survey methodology. At the same time, it also retains many of the advantages of the experimental approach – the ability to measure opinion before and after the Court's decision, to craft measures that closely reflect issues in the decision, and to identify precisely the causal mechanism involved. Natural, or quasi-experiments, expose "subjects" to political information in the same way those individuals receive most of their other political information – from the media, most likely. Furthermore, conducting research in the field enables gathering information from a much more random subset of the population. Both allow for greater generalization of the findings.

While this particular design is the best available method for addressing the questions at hand, it also has its shortcomings. First, it simply is not possible to generalize these results to the entire population of the United States. Furthermore, the studies are limited to a handful of cases, ones that were not chosen randomly. This research does not occur in a controlled environment such as a laboratory, allowing for the possibility that any observed patterns or changes are due to something other than the Court's decisions. This might occur when people talk about the issues with other people, or when people read about the decision in a newspaper editorial, for example.[7]

---

[7] A related problem is that the world, including the world of politics, often provides for natural and interesting manipulations, but these events are almost always totally out of the researcher's control. It is impossible to always know when and how they will occur. In this project, there was no control over when the Supreme Court would hand down its decisions. The timing of oral arguments and the Court's tendency to hand down decisions at the end of the term provides an idea as to what to expect. Most of the decisions were handed down toward the end of the term. But, some events – notably the bombing of the Oklahoma City Federal Building – could not be controlled or even predicted. As it turned out, one of the decisions was handed down the same day as the Oklahoma City bombing. Needless to say, the Court's decision received virtually no media coverage anywhere. In another instance, a decision on a case from Iowa was handed down after less than a week of initial interviewing. These are the kinds of things that are totally out of the researcher's control. Occasionally, research has turned such events to an advantage. An example of such a fortuitous event serves as the basis for Mondak's (1995) book, *Nothing to Read*, where a newspaper strike in Pittsburgh allowed for a comparison of the acquisition of political knowledge during an election campaign. In Pittsburgh, there was no newspaper

Moreover, unlike true experiments, quasi-experimental designs do not allow for testing some interesting hypotheses. In particular, some experimental research includes manipulations to try to understand some of the psychological mechanisms underpinning the findings of change or no change (see Mondak 1990, 1991, 1992, 1994; Segal 1995). Those who study the Supreme Court and public opinion owe an intellectual debt to the experimental research. The development of this project's hypotheses was based on these experimental findings. Clearly, interesting hypotheses will continue to be developed and tested in the laboratory. To some extent then, the studies are replications of the results supported by experimental research. At the same time, this is an instance where replication is no trivial matter, especially since doubts linger about the validity and generalizability of the experimental findings.

SAMPLING

In each of the four studies, two random samples were created of the residents from the communities where the case originated. The first of these samples consists of residents from the *immediate* town. The second is made up of those who reside in the *surrounding* towns. The surrounding area sample tends to reflect the coverage of the dominant local newspaper.[8] Additional information on sampling issues can be found in Appendix A.

For two studies, two additional samples were created. These too were drawn according to town of residence. However, these individuals participated *only* in the second wave of the study. Since participation alone in a panel study may affect those who participate, the second-wave-only samples are included in order to help understand whether participation in the study had any discernible effects on the attitudes of the respondents.[9]

---

coverage of the election; however, in Cleveland, Ohio, a city with similar congressional campaigns, the newspapers did cover the election.

[8] The samples were created using published telephone directories. Therefore, the geographic spread of the samples representing the surrounding communities varies somewhat between the four surveys.

[9] For example, one of the central questions of this book has to do with awareness of Court decisions. It is conceivable that participation in one of the panels may artificially heighten awareness. Those who participate may pay greater attention to the issues than they otherwise would. The subjects in these two samples, who are only contacted after the Court's decision, serve as a control group for such effects. If there are no significant differences between those who participate in both waves and those who participate only in the second wave, then we can safely assume that participation in the study had no effect on the subjects' acquisition of information. The idea for using a control group arose after finding high levels of awareness in the first two studies.

ORGANIZATION OF THE BOOK

The following chapter, Chapter 2, briefly describes the cases that serve as the quasi-experimental manipulations, placing them in a political and legal context. A total of four cases was selected: two civil liberty cases and two economic cases. One case presents a mix of First Amendment issues: free speech, free exercise of religion, and religious establishment (*Lamb's Chapel v. Center Moriches Union Free High School District* [1993]). The second case deals exclusively with a religious establishment controversy (*Board of Education of Kiryas Joel v. Grumet* [1994]). The third case involves state authority to tax the gasoline sold by members of a Native American Indian tribe (*Oklahoma Tax Commission v. Chickasaw Nation* [1995]).[10] The fourth and final case involves a controversy over the federal government's application of the 1973 Endangered Species Act to protect the habitat of endangered and threatened species on private property (*Babbitt, Secretary of the Interior, et al., v. Sweet Home Chapter of Communities for a Great Oregon* [1995]).

One goal of this more detailed discussion is to firmly establish that these are "ordinary" cases, the kinds of cases that should be examined to understand whether there is any general pattern to the effect of Supreme Court decisions on public opinion. But the primary goal of this discussion is to provide information that may anticipate and shed light on the empirical findings in subsequent chapters. The hypotheses, outlined previously in this chapter, are clearly very general. Overall the results should be similar across the studies. That being said, these four cases are very different from each other, as are the communities from which they are drawn. The unique features in each of these cases and communities may, to some extent, mediate or moderate the expected effects.

Chapter 3 begins the empirical analysis of the impact of these Court decisions on public opinion. Specifically, this chapter discusses the quantity and quality of media coverage, knowledge of, and interest in these four Supreme Court decisions. In other words, this chapter tests the *Media Coverage Hypothesis,* the awareness hypotheses (*Local/National Hypothesis* and the *Immediate/Surrounding Hypothesis*), and finally, the *Local Importance Hypothesis.*

If the local media do a good job covering these cases, then it is reasonable to expect the local citizens to have access to this information. So, the

---

[10] This case also involved a question about whether the state of Oklahoma could tax the income of members of the Chickasaw Nation who did not reside or work on Native American land.

first part of the chapter examines the quantity of media coverage, both locally and nationally. The sheer number of stories alone, however, cannot guarantee that the public will have a good understanding of the decision. The reporters need to do a reasonable job conveying that information to the public. Thus, there are also measures of the quality of the local newspapers' coverage of these cases. The second part of this chapter examines whether that critical linking mechanism, the media, was able to inform citizens, and whether this piqued their interest in the issues.

Differences in how strongly the residents of the geographic communities feel about the issue are important since the consensus of research on political attitudes suggests that people who hold strong attitudes are less likely to be persuaded, even by the Supreme Court. Those who feel strongly about the issue should be less likely to change their opinion following the Court's decision, but more likely to change how they feel about the Court. These questions are explored in more detail in Chapters 4 and 5.

Chapter 4 begins the examination of whether the Court's decisions had any effect on public opinion. This chapter focuses on testing the hypotheses about any changes in respondents' attitudes as a result of the Court's decision (*Opinion Change/Town of Residence Hypothesis*, *Opinion Change/Court Support Hypothesis*, and the *Town/Court Support Interaction Hypothesis*). The analysis is conducted at the individual level using both bivariate and multivariate techniques with change in attitude toward the issue as the dependent variable.

This final empirical chapter, Chapter 5, examines the hypotheses about how the content of the Court's decision affects support for the Court (*Change in Support for the Court Hypothesis*, *Town of Residence/Support for Court Interaction*). The analysis in this chapter is conducted at the individual level using multivariate regression techniques with change in support for the Court as the dependent variable. Included in this analysis are other variables, such as how strongly the person felt about the issue, and the individual's geographic proximity to the case.

The concluding chapter, Chapter 6, summarizes the main findings and discusses the meaning in relation to the Court's role in the United States constitutional system. The discussion focuses particularly on the implications that the Court's political capital appears expendable and that people appear to evaluate the Court based on its actions.

The chapter also challenges the widely held view that most Americans are uninformed about political issues and do not make meaningful connections between issues. However, where the media provided extensive information, public awareness followed. While most citizens held their ground on the issues, some updated their view of the Court in response to those decisions.

Finally, the chapter explores areas where future research should head in light of these results. First and foremost, future research needs to discover whether we can extend the findings to other kinds of populations based on, for example, occupation, religion, or social, civic, and cultural interests. There is good reason to believe that there are many other groups, not just geographic, where access to information and interest in Supreme Court cases is high enough to produce similar results. In addition, future research might go back to the experimental lab. Since so many of our hypotheses are developed from experimental research, in what other fruitful directions might this research lead us? Finally, rather than abandon the examination of national level effects, more emphasis should be placed on designing better national surveys.

2

From the Marble Temple to Main Street

Placing the Cases in Political and Legal Context

The previous chapter introduced the research questions and the specific hypotheses investigated in this book along with the research strategy used to answer these questions and hypotheses. However, the four cases that serve as the quasi-experimental manipulations have been referred to simply as ordinary cases – ones that represent the bulk of the Court's day-to-day, term-to-term work. The hypotheses have also been presented to suggest that these cases are similar, or at least that the expectations are similar. While this is all true – these are ordinary cases, and the hypotheses should provide a general explanation of the impact of Court decisions on local public opinion – it should be equally clear that in the world of politics, nothing is ever quite equal. Each case is unique. These attributes – the issues, communities, and history – may ultimately affect the individual local communities in distinctive ways.

Although social science research strives to provide general theories and common explanations, it should also note the features of individual cases. These attributes, which often account for deviations from the predicted and general patterns, may be useful for modifying existing theories and developing new hypotheses. The following pages provide a detailed description of the individual cases, the background of the controversies, the communities where they evolved, and the actual Court decisions; this information should prove useful in anticipating and explaining the empirical results presented in the subsequent chapters.

Although this chapter focuses on the differences of these cases, there are also many things in common. In fact, these four cases are truly representative of the Court's docket. While they may not have national political or legal significance, like most of the Court's work, these cases present a conflict important enough for the parties to continue the case through the court system, and significant enough for the Court to render a definitive answer. As far as legal doctrine is concerned, most of these cases simply clarify how the Court's past decisions apply to the current controversies. Therefore, they are not remarkable in the development of the Court's doctrine. These ordinary decisions, the ones often overlooked in research on the Court and public opinion, are precisely the ones that should be studied. It would be surprising if cases such as *Brown* or *Roe* did *not* have an impact on public opinion. Indeed, research has shown they clearly have (Franklin and Kosaki 1989; Johnson and Martin 1998). As interesting, and probably more consequential, is the question of whether more routine cases can have an effect, and whether the effect differs from extraordinary cases.

Four cases are included in the analysis. Two cases involve civil liberty claims. The first, the Center Moriches case, involves a host of First Amendment issues: free exercise of religion, free speech, and religious establishment. The second case, the Monroe case, involves a religious establishment controversy exclusively. The other two cases are somewhat more difficult to categorize. One involves a dispute over taxes and the other over the use of private property. Both are classified as economic cases, but there are other, noneconomic dimensions to these cases. The Oklahoma case, involving state taxation of Native Americans, obviously involves Native Americans. Therefore, some scholars might also treat this as having a civil rights dimension.[1] The Oregon case, involving interpretation and application of the Endangered Species Act, primarily has an effect on the community's business interests and private property owners, but it also includes an obvious environmental dimension. For the most part, though, these last two cases involve economic disputes. Both of these issues, civil liberties and economics, continue to dominate the Court's attentions over the last fifty years (Pacelle 1991). In addition to representing a range of substantive issues, the cases also represent a geographic range. This too should increase the generalizability of the findings. Two of the cases come from the state of New York (one from Long Island and the other from upstate New York), one from Oklahoma, and finally, one from Oregon.

---

[1] In the coding scheme of the Supreme Court Judicial Database, Harold Spaeth codes issues involving Native Americans under the civil rights category.

THE FOUR CASES: HISTORY, CONTEXT, AND COURT DECISIONS

The remainder of this chapter briefly describes the background of these controversies, the communities from where they originate, and the Supreme Court's decision. Although each case ends up on the Court's docket, their paths to the Court's bench are very different. Some represent issues that the communities have struggled with for long periods of time; some are more recent, but intense; and others represent issues that sprang up quickly. Some cases have had more of a direct impact on the material self-interests of residents, while the others are less connected to the material well being of the local residents. Moreover, some of these issues and controversies continued for some time after the Court's ruling, while others quickly fell off the legal and political landscape. The differences in these stories might be important to understanding the extent of national and local media coverage of these cases, local levels of awareness, opinion change on the issues in the cases, and change in support for the Court – the topics of Chapters 3, 4, and 5. At the very least, they provide important information about the context of these controversies.

The First Amendment/Religion Cases

Center Moriches

The first controversy emerged from Center Moriches, a relatively small community of fewer than 6,000 residents located on the eastern end of Long Island, along its southern shores. The immediate community sample is made up of residents from Center Moriches, and the surrounding community sample is made up of residents from the surrounding communities of Suffolk County. Both Center Moriches and the surrounding communities in Suffolk County are predominantly white and moderately well educated. The residents of Suffolk County as a whole are slightly better off financially than are the residents of Center Moriches.[2] The relatively small population of Center Moriches supports only two schools, an elementary school and a high school. It is in the high school's auditorium where the drama emerges.

---

[2] Both Suffolk County and Center Moriches are about 90 percent white. In Center Moriches, about 94 percent have at least a high school education and about 21.5 percent have at least a four-year college degree. In Suffolk County, about 82 percent have at least a high school education and about 23 percent have a bachelor's degree. The median income in Center Moriches in 1989 was $42,737 and in Suffolk County it was about $49,128 (Bureau of the Census 1990).

The case that emerges from this otherwise unremarkable suburb, *Lamb's Chapel v. Center Moriches Union Free School District*, began on November 11, 1988, when Reverend John Steigerwald, the pastor of a local church, asked to use the local high school's auditorium for religious services and instruction on Sunday afternoons. The church, Lamb's Chapel, is a nondenominational church with a membership of around 150 people. While nondenominational, the church is affiliated with Fellowship of Christian Assemblies, which has its roots in the Pentecostal movement and the Baptist religion. The school board declined the request.

Next, Steigerwald submitted a written request to use the same facilities, this time in order to show a six-part film, "Turn Your Heart Toward Home," a film about family values – with indisputable religious overtones. The film featured a psychologist discussing parenting and family issues from a religious point of view, emphasizing a need to return to religious values. Steigerwald sent the first written request to the school board on December 16, 1988. The school board rejected both requests on the grounds "...that plaintiff's use of the facilities appeared to be for a religious purpose" but requested more information from Steigerwald in order to make a final determination (736 F. Supp.1247, 1990 at 1250). Steigerwald sent the board a brochure about the film. Again they rejected his request because the film "appear[ed] to be church related" (736 F. Supp.1247, 1990 at 1251). Steigerwald resubmitted his request the following October and, once again, the board denied the request for the same reason.

The school board based its decision on both New York law (§414 of the New York Education Law) and the school board's own rules relating to that law (Rule No. 7 of the school district's Rules and Regulations for Community Use of School Facilities). Specifically, state law authorizes local school districts to allow certain groups access to school premises after school hours for "social, civic, and recreational meetings and entertainments, but the list of permitted uses does not include meetings for religious purposes" (quoted in 508 U.S. 384, at 384). The school district rules (i.e., Rule No. 7) allow the facilities to be used for civic, social, and recreational purposes, but they specifically prohibit the use of the property for religious purposes.

The school district's superintendent, Joseph Donovan, claimed that New York law and the First Amendment made his decision to deny the request straightforward. He believed that allowing the church access to show an obviously religiously motivated film would not only violate state law, but would also violate the First Amendment's prohibition against religious establishment. On the other hand, Steigerwald felt that the school district's decision discriminated against the church, since other community groups – the Girl Scouts, the Salvation Army youth band, a gospel choir, and others – were allowed access.

Lamb's Chapel hired a local lawyer and sued the school board in a federal district court, claiming the school district's decision violated the free speech and assembly, free exercise of religion, and religious establishment clauses of the First Amendment, as applied to the states through the due process clause of the Fourteenth Amendment. The school board also hired a local lawyer for this first round in the courts and they were supported by the New York State School Board Association which submitted an *amicus curiae* brief on their behalf.

The district court ruled against the church on July 15, 1991. The church appealed. At this point, Pat Robertson's legal foundation, the American Center for Law and Justice and Concerned Women for America, a prominent and conservative Christian group, provided the church with lawyers and legal support for the duration of the appeals.[3] Even so, the Court of Appeals upheld the district court's decision against the church. The church and its lawyers filed a petition with the Supreme Court, which accepted the case for review and heard oral arguments in February of 1993. The Supreme Court unanimously overturned the Court of Appeals – ruling in favor of the church – in its June 7, 1993, decision.

Justice Byron White's opinion for the unanimous Court focused mainly on the free speech element of the controversy. The school district, according to White, would have been well within its rights not to open its doors for community use. Once they did, they would even be allowed, as their rule states, to close the school doors for religious purposes. But, according to Justice White, that is not what they did. Instead, they closed their doors

---

[3] The American Center for Law and Justice and Jay Sekulow were the attorneys in the following Supreme Court cases: *Board of Airport Commissioners v. Jews for Jesus* (1987), *United States v. Kokinda* (1990), *Board of Ed. of Westside Comm. Schools v. Mergens* (1990), *ISKCON v. Lee* (1992), *Bray v. Alexandria Women's Health Clinic* (1993), *Schenck v. Pro-Choice Network of Western New York* (1997), *Hill v. Colorado* (2000), *Santa Fe Independent School District v. Doe* (2000). Some of the recent cases on which they have acted as amicus include: *Boy Scouts of America v. Dale* (2000), *Mitchell v. Helms* (2000), *Sternberg, et al. v. Carhart, M.D.* (2000), *Troxel v. Granville* (2000), *Vacco v. Quill* (1997), *Washington v. Glucksberg* (1997), *City of Borne, Texas v. Flores* (1997), *Capital Square Review, et al., v. Vincent J. Pinette, et al.* (1993), *Ronald W. Rosenberger, et al., v. The Rectors and Visitors of the University of Virginia* (1995), *Madsen, et al. v. Women's Health Center Inc., et al.* (1994), *Kiryas Joel Village School District v. Louis Grumet* (1994), *Zobrest v. Catalina Foothills School District* (1993).

to a film on family life and child rearing – topics that fall within their own guidelines. The viewpoint on family values expressed in the film was a religious one, but the topic itself was permissible. In other words, they discriminated against the church based on its viewpoint. White largely dismissed the religious establishment issue by writing that "... there would be no realistic danger that the community would think that the District was endorsing religion or any particular creed, and any benefit to religion or the Church would have been incidental." Justices Antonin Scalia and Anthony Kennedy wrote concurring opinions.[4]

So, at the end of years of legal battles, the church, represented by the lawyers from the American Center for Law and Justice, and Concerned Women for America, was allowed to show its film. Unlike some of the other controversies, there were no lingering ramifications from the decision. The school board did not make any attempts to block the decision, and there was little protest among the local residents.

As the next chapter shows, although there was substantial media coverage of the decision, it was not as intense as for other cases in this study. Other than the immediate coverage of the controversy following the Court's decision, there were only occasional mentions in the local paper prior to the actual decision. Even so, this brief media attention produced surprisingly high levels of knowledge among members of the local population. Once the Court handed down the decision, the church quickly retired from the public limelight, and has not been the subject of any controversies since then. Quite a different picture emerges just one year later in the case from Monroe Township where underlying tensions existed for years, and the Court's decision failed to end the controversy.

Monroe

The other civil liberties case comes from the relatively small town of Monroe, which is situated in upstate New York, about 60 miles north of Manhattan, in the predominantly Republican Orange County. Monroe Township is composed of two villages, the Village of Monroe and the

---

[4] Justice Scalia's separate opinion concurred with the Court's decision but criticized the continued use of the *Lemon* test (from *Lemon v. Kurtzman* 1971) and the endorsement approach. Instead, he would hold that granting access to the church to show the film does not violate the establishment clause for the simple reason that such an action does not signify an "embrace" or preference for this particular religious sect. Justice Clarence Thomas joined his opinion. Justice Kennedy's concurring opinion states essentially the same thing.

Village of Kiryas Joel. The separation of this town into two villages is
an important part of the story. However, for the purposes of sampling
and the comparisons made in subsequent chapters, both Monroe and
Kiryas Joel are included in the immediate community sample, and the
surrounding towns and communities of Orange County provide the
surrounding community sample.

Like the Center Moriches case, this one is also about a First Amendment
dispute. Although Center Moriches and Monroe are located just a few
hours from each other, the communities and the dispute in these two cases
are worlds apart. The Monroe controversy has a long and divisive history,
one that predates the specific case that winds up on the Court's docket. In
addition, once the Supreme Court hands down the decision in this case, the
tensions do not disappear. Rather, the legal and political battles at the heart
of the dispute continue for years. There are also important differences
between these geographic regions. While Center Moriches is a microcosm
of the larger Suffolk County, there are considerable differences between
the various communities within Orange County, where the Monroe case
emerged.

The Supreme Court case is just one dispute in a long line of legal battles
and general tensions between the residents of the Village of Monroe and
the Village of Kiryas Joel. The specific case, *Board of Education of Kiryas
Joel v. Grumet*, concerns whether New York's state legislature's creation
of a special school district for a Hasidic Jewish community, specifically
the Village of Kiryas Joel, violated the First Amendment's prohibition
against religious establishment. But to really understand this specific dispute, it is necessary to put it in context of the ongoing tensions in this
community.

Some of these issues undoubtedly arise from the cultural differences.
The Hasidim, an ultra-orthodox sect of Judaism, maintain a lifestyle alien
to mainstream Americans. The men wear only black clothing, always wear
a yarmulke and wide-brimmed hats, and grow long beards and side locks.
The women dress very modestly in long-sleeved shirts and long skirts, and
married women must cover their hair – usually with a wig. Women are
not allowed to drive and married women, except on rare occasions, do
not work outside of the home. The family size in Kiryas Joel is almost
twice as large as it is in Monroe.[5] The residents of Monroe, and the
surrounding communities in Orange County, are substantially better off

---

[5] According to the 1990 U.S. Census, the average family size for residents of Kiryas Joel is
6.52 and 3.43 in the Village of Monroe.

financially than are the residents of Kiryas Joel.[6] This disparity in family size and income has led to the perception, not completely unfounded, that the members of Kiryas Joel rely heavily on public assistance. Some figures show that more than 70 percent of the residents of Kiryas Joel receive some form of public assistance including Medicaid, food stamps, or welfare (*The New York Times*, 4 September 1986). The communities differ on another important dimension – education. The residents of Monroe and the rest of Orange County in general are much better educated than are the residents of Kiryas Joel.[7]

In addition to these more generalized cultural, religious, and economic tensions, there have also been many specific disputes. The first conflicts arose over zoning regulations. Monroe was zoned for single-family occupancy, but, among the Hasidim, typically multiple, and usually large, families occupied single homes (*The New York Times*, 20 October 1976). The ultimate resolution was to divide Monroe Township into two separate villages – Monroe and Kiryas Joel. In May of 1985, the conflict between these communities was reawakened when two members of Kiryas Joel ran for seats on the Monroe-Woodbury school board. They did so even though the vast majority of the children from Kiryas Joel attended private schools.[8] Many residents of the Village of Monroe saw this as an attempt to take over the school board and so they initiated a highly publicized campaign (*The New York Times*, 20 October 1976). Again, in the mid-1980s approximately 600 boys who attended a Hasidic school refused to board school buses driven by women since the Hasidim believe that the sexes should be separate.

A conflict between the Hasidim's religious beliefs and the local schools ultimately wound up at the Supreme Court. While the majority of the Hasidic children attended private schools, paid for and run by the community itself, the community was unable to provide appropriate services for the approximately 200 children in need of special education. Most parents were opposed to sending their children to the special education

---

[6] While the median household income, as measured in the 1990 Census, is $47,609 for the residents of the Village of Monroe, it is only $14,702 for the residents of the Village of Kiryas Joel. In the remainder of Orange County, the median income is $39,198.

[7] In Kiryas Joel only about 48 percent of the adults (over age 25) have a high school diploma, and only about 6 percent have earned a bachelor's degree. In Monroe, about 82 percent have at least a high school diploma, and about 25 percent have at least a bachelor's degree. In the surrounding communities of Orange County about 77 percent have at least a high school diploma and nearly 20 percent have at least a bachelor's degree.

[8] Although they had separated to resolve the zoning conflicts, they remained joined together in a single school district.

programs in the public schools in order to avoid interactions with children from outside their community. Many of these parents were so adamantly opposed that they removed their children from school entirely. This prompted the state legislature to establish a special public school district for the community in 1989. The newly created Kiryas Joel School District consisted of only one school which was designed to meet the needs of this single group of children with special needs.

The creation of the school district was somewhat controversial at the outset. Although the plan encountered very little opposition in the state legislature (*The New York Times*, 26 July 1989), it was opposed by many groups, including the New York Civil Liberties Union, the American Jewish Congress, the State Education Department, and the state School Boards Association. These groups lobbied then-Governor Mario Cuomo to veto the bill. However, under pressure from the Hasidic communities in Kiryas Joel and Brooklyn, Governor Cuomo signed the bill into law, arguing that it was a "practical solution to an intractable problem" (*The New York Times*, 26 July 1989, B4).

Even before the school opened its doors, Luis Grumet, head of the New York State School Boards Association, filed suit against the school district in a state trial court. Grumet argued that the school district impermissibly advanced a particular religious interest, thereby violating the religious establishment clause.[9] The trial court agreed and the decision was upheld by an intermediate court of appeals and the New York Court of Appeals (the highest court in New York). The school district appealed to the Supreme Court, which accepted the case and heard oral arguments on March 30, 1994. On June 27, 1994, the Supreme Court voted six to three that the creation of the school district did indeed violate the First Amendment prohibition on the establishment of religion.

Writing for the majority, Justice David Souter maintained that the creation of the school district was unconstitutional for two reasons: first, it delegated state functions to a religious group; and second, it was not neutral between religious groups. As for granting state functions to a religious group, Souter relied on a previous Court case, *Larkin v. Grendel's Den, Inc.* (1982), where the Court decided that states may not confer governmental functions to religious groups.[10] As for the neutrality issue,

---

[9] Interestingly, but probably not coincidentally, Luis Grumet submitted an *amicus curiae* brief on behalf of the School Board in the Center Moriches case.

[10] In *Larkin*, the Court was asked to decide whether a Massachusetts law allowing churches to decide whether nearby restaurants would be granted liquor licenses violated the establishment clause. In an eight-to-one vote (with Rehnquist dissenting) Burger, writing for the majority, finds that giving such powers to a religious institution "enmeshes

Souter wrote that the case-specific nature of the New York law creating the school district did not guarantee that other religious communities would be entitled to similar treatment. Additionally, the majority argued there were other ways the state could protect and educate the Hasidic children without creating a special school district. For example, the existing public school district could have provided appropriate programs either in existing facilities or at a neutral site.[11] There were four separate opinions in this case – one dissenting and three concurring opinions.

Despite the Court's decision, the controversy did not end. Quite the contrary. Virtually the following day, state legislators converged on Albany in order to figure out a way to get around the ruling. They quickly enacted similar legislation which was also thrown out by the New York Court of Appeals, again on religious establishment grounds. A third law was enacted in 1997. In its attempt to appear neutral, the legislature did not specifically mention Kiryas Joel in this third piece of legislation. However, even though it appeared facially neutral, it too was thrown out by the New York Court of Appeals since only Kiryas Joel and one other small village in upstate New York would have benefitted. The state appealed to the Supreme Court, but in 1999, the Court refused to accept the case for review.[12] The legislature has since attempted another version of the law, one that as of 2002 was still in litigation.

Given the nature of the dispute – both the background and the legislature's response – it seemed plausible to expect the local media to pay significant attention to this controversy. In fact, there might be intense coverage at many points: before the Court's decision, immediately following the decision, and possibly for some time afterward as the legislature convened to address the issue. It is reasonable to expect such intense coverage because the Hasidim are very visible in the community and have found themselves at the center of previous legal and political disputes.

---

churches in the exercise of substantial governmental powers contrary to . . . First Amendment" prohibitions against religious establishment (quoted in Abraham and Perry 1998, 309).

[11] The division among the justices was similar to the Center Moriches Case. Justices Blackmun and Stevens filed concurring opinions. Justice O'Connor filed an opinion concurring in part and concurring in the judgment. Justice Kennedy filed an opinion concurring in the judgment. Justice Scalia filed a dissenting opinion joined by Chief Justice Rehnquist and Justice Thomas. In other words, the justices were just as divided over the reasoning behind this religious establishment case as they appear to be on most establishment cases recently. Unlike the Center Moriches case, though, this one did not even create unanimity around the outcome.

[12] The case, *Pataki v. Grumet* 98-1932, received only three votes for certiorari (from Justices O'Connor, Scalia, and Thomas).

Additionally, the local paper, *The Times Herald-Record*, has covered the community extensively in the past.[13] Thus, there is every reason to suspect that the local versus national media coverage hypothesis should perform particularly well in this specific case.

The ongoing nature of the dispute might also be important to consider in terms of the hypotheses about the importance of this issue to the local residents, whether they are likely to change their opinion on this issue, and whether the decision has any effect on their confidence in the Court. Since this issue is just one of many controversies between residents of these communities, it is reasonable to expect the local residents will attach a great deal of significance to this specific issue, even more so than in some of the other cases. This expectation is further buttressed by the fact that as the next chapter reveals, there was extensive media coverage of the case.

Moreover, given the numerous other instances of conflict between these two communities, attitudes may have been fairly well established among members of the local community (and maybe even among residents of the surrounding community) long before this specific controversy emerged. So, the Court might have even less of an effect on the attitudes of the immediate community members than it does in the other cases. Even among those in the surrounding communities – who should be more likely to change their opinions in response to the Court's decision – there may have been enough prior information to insulate them from the persuasive context of the Court's decision. On the other hand, the divisiveness and history of the issue may actually heighten the effects of the Court's decision. In this case, the Court's decision might actually have a substantial effect on subsequent evaluations of the Court.

The Economic Cases

Oklahoma
The third case is *Oklahoma Tax Commission v. Chickasaw Nation*. The question in this case was whether or not the state of Oklahoma could collect tax on gasoline sold by Native Americans on tribal land.[14] The state of Oklahoma is no stranger to disputes with Native American tribes,

---

[13] A simple search of the newspaper's archive over the last few decades produced literally hundreds of stories about the community and its members.

[14] This case also involved a question of whether the state of Oklahoma could tax the income of members of the Chickasaw Nation who did not reside or work on Native American land. Because the primary issue was the gasoline tax, the analysis focuses on that issue alone.

especially disputes over the imposition of state taxes. Of all the states, Oklahoma has the largest Native American population.[15] So it should come as little surprise that the state and the various tribes are often embroiled in legal disputes. In fact, in this specific case, there were thirteen Native American owned gasoline outlets in Oklahoma, but only two were owned by members of the Chickasaw Nation. In monetary terms, both the Choctaw and Cherokee tribes paid more taxes than did the two Chickasaw stations. However, the Chickasaw Nation challenged the tax.

The town of Ada, headquarters of the Chickasaw Nation, is about 80 miles southeast of Oklahoma City in Pontotoc County. The population of Ada in 1990 was approximately 16,000, about 2,100 of whom are Native American, mostly members of the Chickasaw Nation.[16] Ada serves as the immediate community sample for this case. The majority of the surrounding community sample is drawn from Oklahoma County, which includes Oklahoma City and its outlying communities. Both the immediate and surrounding communities are all within the same market of the major local paper (*The Daily Oklahoman*).

Although both counties, Pontotoc and Oklahoma, are in the same media market, they differ in some important ways. Oklahoma County tends to be strongly Republican, while Pontotoc County is more strongly Democratic. There are some differences in median income: Oklahoma County residents are the best off financially, then residents of Pontotoc County, followed last by residents of Ada. But, there are almost no differences between these communities in terms of educational achievement.[17]

In Oklahoma, there are no reservations. Instead, members of tribes, like any other citizens of the state, own land privately. The tribe itself holds

---

[15] Approximately 8 percent of the state's population is Native American; and, there are thirty-nine tribes headquartered in the state.

[16] Chickasaws do not live exclusively in Ada, but the majority do reside in the south central part of the state. Ada is considered the Chickasaw Nation's home. The tribe's governor and legislature are in Ada, which is also the center of the tribe's cultural and economic activities (*The Daily Oklahoman*, 30 July 1994).

[17] The 1989 median household income in the city of Ada was $15,795. It was slightly higher in the rest of Pontotoc County ($17,945), and still higher in Oklahoma County ($26,129). Educational achievement actually varies little between these different communities. In Ada, approximately 71 percent have at least a high school diploma, and about 23 percent have at least a bachelor's degree. In Pontotoc, the figures are about 69 percent and 18 percent respectively. And in Oklahoma County, the numbers are 79 percent and 23 percent.

about 2,200 acres in a land trust. The combination of tribal sovereignty (despite the lack of clear geographic boundaries between tribe and state) and the large Native American population have led to somewhat frequent legal disputes between the many different tribes and the state of Oklahoma. For example, in the early part of the 1990s, there was another controversy surrounding the collection of state taxes, specifically a statewide tax on tobacco. The Chickasaws and other tribes sold cigarettes without charging the tax. In 1991, the Supreme Court ruled that tribes would have to collect taxes on cigarettes sold to people who are not members of the tribes; however, the Court did not provide any feasible way for the state to enforce the ruling without interfering with tribal sovereignty (*Daily Oklahoman*, 23 April 1995). When the tribes realized that Congress could enact legislation enabling states to impose taxes on all cigarettes sold by the tribes, the Chickasaws and many others voluntarily entered into an agreement allowing the state to collect a smaller tax.

The specific controversy began when the Oklahoma Tax Commission, under pressure from lobbying efforts on behalf of other gasoline station owners, decided to enforce the collection of gasoline tax from members of the tribe who own and operate service stations. The tax amounted to seventeen cents per gallon of gasoline and fourteen cents per gallon of diesel fuel. The non-Native American business owners felt this placed them at a disadvantage if they had to pass the tax on to consumers while the Native American- owned stations did not. The state argued that since virtually all of the state's income for roads and highways comes from gasoline taxes, and since all residents of the state – including Native Americans – use the roads and benefit from their maintenance, the tribes should also pay into the fund. The state also noted that such an imposition would have no effect on tribal sovereignty. The Chickasaws refused to pay; so in 1991, the Oklahoma Tax Commission sued the Chickasaw Nation in federal district court to collect the unpaid taxes. The district court decided in favor of the state of Oklahoma, but the Court of Appeals for the Tenth Circuit reversed the district court's decision. Finally, on June 14, 1995, the Supreme Court unanimously decided that the state of Oklahoma could not collect the gasoline tax.

In her opinion for the Court, Justice Ruth Bader Ginsburg relied on the fact that Congress had not acted to authorize the state of Oklahoma to collect such taxes. The decision emphasized that the imposition of the gasoline tax would be placed on the retailer, in this case members of the tribe, not on the consumer or distributor. This distinction was crucial to the Court. In cases where the Court has found the burden of taxation lies mostly on Native Americans, the Court has decided *against* the state.

As with the Monroe case, the Court's decision did not completely end the debate over this issue. State legislators immediately went to work to determine how to collect the tax, yet abide by the Court's decision. Oklahoma Governor Frank Keating proposed legislation placing the burden directly on the consumer (*The Daily Oklahoman*, 21 June 1995). Groups representing the non-Native American businesses were opposed to such a plan and argued that, similar to the tobacco tax problem, it would be impossible for the state to enforce such a policy because of tribal sovereignty. In May of 1996, the state legislature finally passed a bill allowing tribes to enter voluntarily into a compact with the state. According to the terms of the compact, tribes would agree to pay the seventeen-cent tax when they purchase the gasoline. The state would give back 3 percent. In addition, any tribe agreeing to these terms – regardless of whether they actually operate a filling station – would receive $25,000 a year.

The fact that this case involves taxation might affect expectations in subsequent chapters. Most importantly is that taxes tend to be an issue most people consider to be of relatively low salience. Slotnick and Segal (1998), for example, suggest that all else equal, tax cases tend to be infrequently covered in the media. First, they are often technical and not as easily conveyed or understood. Second, they do not tend to capture public interest. While there should be greater media coverage by members of the local media than the national media (consistent with the *Media Coverage Hypothesis*), especially since the case involves a locally recognizable group, overall media coverage should be lower than in the other cases, and thus, levels of awareness should be lower as well.

However, the other hypotheses about the public's awareness of the case should behave as predicted: people in the immediate community should exhibit higher levels of awareness than those in the surrounding communities. Although both communities have the same opportunity to learn about the case, the fact that this case involves a recognizable group from the immediate community should heighten interest among the residents of Ada. Similarly, the residents of Ada should find this case to be more important than would residents from the surrounding communities. The expectations remain the same for the the hypotheses about opinion change and change in evaluation of the Court. Among those who hear about the decision, those from the surrounding communities should show greater opinion change in support of the Court's ruling and those from the immediate community should be more likely to update their views of the Supreme Court.

Oregon

The fourth case, *Babbitt, Secretary of the Interior, et al. v. Sweet Home Chapter of Communities for a Great Oregon,* began in Sweet Home, Oregon, a small logging community about 85 miles south of Portland. The main industry in this town of about 7,000 people is the timber industry – both logging and milling – and has been since the 1940s (*Oregonian,* 1 December 1990). For sampling purposes, the residents of Sweet Home are included in the immediate community sample. Due to the nature of the local media market, the surrounding community sample includes the residents of Linn County, which encompasses Sweet Home, and Multnomah County, which includes the city of Portland. There are important differences between these communities. Overall, the residents of Sweet Home are both less educated and worse off financially than are those who live in the surrounding communities – especially the residents of Multnomah County.[18]

These differences aside, like many other small towns in rural Oregon, Sweet Home's economy revolves around logging and milling. Beginning in the 1980s, the logging industry started to experience some serious hardships. Some of the early problems were purely a function of overall poor economic times; but these problems were exacerbated by the growing conservation and environmental movements' efforts to halt logging in the old-growth forests of the Pacific Northwest.

The specific case included in this book is about the interpretation of the Endangered Species Act (ESA). The Fish and Wildlife Service (which falls under the auspices of the U.S. Department of Interior and then-Secretary of the Interior Bruce Babbit) translated the Act as protecting the habitat of the endangered spotted owl, which makes its home in the old growth trees in the Pacific Northwest. This broad interpretation, protecting not only individual animals but their habitats as well, had major consequences for the timber industry as it effectively set aside large sections of old growth forests on both public and private land.

---

[18] Only about 61 percent of the residents of Sweet Home have a high school diploma, and less than 7 percent have a bachelor's degree. In Linn County, about 76 percent have at least a high school diploma and about 11 percent have a bachelor's degree. In Multnomah County, which includes the city of Portland, 83 percent have at least a high school diploma and fully 24 percent have at least a bachelor's degree. The median household income in Sweet Home in 1989 was $18,685. In Linn and Multnomah counties, the median household income in 1989 was $25,209 and $26,928 respectively.

The year 1989 was a particularly bad year for Sweet Home. Three of the eight mills permanently closed their doors. The owners of the mills mentioned several economic factors, but also cited court orders and anticipated lawsuits over the future of the spotted owl as reasons for throwing in the towel in Sweet Home (*The Oregonian*, 14 July 1989). In order to fight the environmental lobby, timber industry groups, local chambers of commerce, labor unions, and The Oregon Project (organized under the Western States Public Lands Coalition, a Colorado-based interest group) all worked to organize local grass-roots organizations (*The Oregonian*, 22 May 1989). Their initial efforts included organizing town hall style meetings, bringing voter registration material, and urging local residents to contact their elected officials (*The Oregonian*, 22 May 1989). In addition, they initiated a local yellow ribbon campaign, encouraging people to display yellow ribbons from their homes, vehicles, and shops to show support for the logging industry (*The Oregonian*, 14 July 1989). In Sweet Home, the yellow ribbon campaign went a step further. Loggers began to place yellow dots on the cash they spent as a tangible symbol of their importance to the local economy. These grass-roots efforts, however, did not have much success. The environmentalists, on the other hand, were winning important victories. In April of 1990, a panel of scientists recommended that millions of acres of old growth forest be set aside for owl habitat (*The Associated Press*, 14 April 1990). This drastically reduced the forest area available for logging.

In June of 1990, the U.S. Fish and Wildlife Service listed the spotted owl as a "threatened species, concluding that logging of federal lands in the Northwest has severely fragmented the aging forests where the bird dwells" (*U.P.I.*, 19 September 1990). This listing provided the grounds not only for judges to set aside federal forests, but also, and more importantly, for barring logging on private property as well.

The logging communities took the matter to court. They argued that Congress never intended the Endangered Species Act to protect the *habitat* of endangered species.[19] They challenged this broad interpretation in a

---

[19] Specifically, the Endangered Species Act makes it unlawful for any person to "take" endangered or threatened species. Section 3(19) of the Act defines the word "take" as follows: "The term 'take' means to harass, harm, pursue, hunt, shoot, wound, kill, capture, or collect, or to attempt to engage in any such conduct" (16 U.S.C. §1532[19]). None of these words were further defined by Congress, but the Department of the Interior (specifically the Fish and Wildlife Service), which is the agency responsible for implementing the regulation, defined "harm" to include significant and detrimental habitat modification. They also cited the wording of the original Senate version of

federal district court. The court agreed with the Fish and Wildlife Service interpretation; but, the Court of Appeals reversed that decision, siding with the business interests and property owners.

Ultimately, though, on June 29, 1995, the Supreme Court decided, by a six-to-three vote, that the habitat of the endangered species is protected by the wording of the 1973 Act. Justice John Paul Stevens delivered the opinion of the Court. Babbitt's broad interpretation was justified, according to Stevens, first, because it was a reasonable interpretation. If modifying the habitat will cause harm to the species, then the habitat must be protected as well. He stated that dictionary definitions of the word "harm," as well as the context of the ESA, support that interpretation. Second, he relies on the legislative intent behind the ESA, and prior Court decisions interpreting that intent. Stevens' understanding of that intent supported Babbitt's position that the purpose of the ESA was to help preserve endangered and threatened species, a goal impossible to achieve without habitat protection. To the majority, this proved that Congress intended to protect the habitat when creating the ESA.[20] There were two separate opinions – a dissent by Justice Antonin Scalia and a concurring opinion by Justice Sandra Day O'Connor.

The debate between the logging interests and the environmentalists in the Pacific Northwest is surely one of the most divisive issues in that

---

the Endangered Species Act, which included a section on habitat modification, that was subsequently removed. To the respondents, this implied that Congress, or at least the Senate, did not intend for a broad interpretation. They also argued that Congress intended to protect endangered species from habitat modification on private property by purchasing that land rather than by regulating what private property owners could do with their property. Finally, they argued that courts should give the narrowest possible interpretation of the word "harm" in the legislation since there was so little debate on it to serve as reference.

[20] He cites §2 of the Act, which states that the main purpose of the Act is to "provide a means whereby the ecosystems upon which endangered species and threatened species depend may be conserved..." (16 U.S.C. §1531 [b]). He also refers to committee reports from both the House and the Senate. The records of both chambers suggest that the intent was to prohibit both direct and indirect harm to endangered species, and that the word "take" was to be interpreted broadly. Finally, Stevens notes that in 1982, Congress amended the Act to allow the Secretary of the Interior to issue permits to people whose actions might otherwise be a prohibited "taking" of an endangered species if it is an incidental "taking" and they can provide a conservation plan that shows how they will mitigate and minimize the potential negative impact on an endangered or threatened species. To Stevens and his colleagues in the majority, this suggests that Congress intended to prohibit both direct and indirect harm to the species. Why? They deduced that the permit process was intended for those whose actions might have an indirect effect on an endangered or threatened species.

region. Even though this issue is certainly an economic one, and economic cases typically garner less media attention (Slotnick and Segal 1998), it would be reasonable to expect a great deal of coverage of this case. Although some of the legal issues are complicated, the spotted owl is a vivid image to accompany a news story. In addition, it is reasonable to expect the residents of these communities to be interested in learning about the Supreme Court decision, giving the media reason to pay more attention to this issue than it does for economic cases in general. Furthermore, as the media coverage hypothesis predicts, there should be even greater coverage of this case locally than nationally.

It is also likely that the residents of the immediate community, those most likely affected by the decision, will feel more strongly about this issue and attach more significance to this case than those from the surrounding communities. Much like the Monroe case, where the dispute and its antecedents had been in play for some time, it is logical to expect the Court to have a more difficult time changing public opinion on this issue. Conversely, because residents probably had preexisting attitudes about this issue, the Court's decision might be an important factor in subsequent evaluations of the Court, especially among immediate community members more directly affected by the outcome.

CONCLUSION

This chapter presented the issues and individual characteristics of the cases. The Center Moriches case involved groups who were previously not very salient in the community. Once the Supreme Court decided that the school board could not discriminate based on viewpoint, the controversy quickly and quietly disappeared. On the other end of the spectrum were two cases with visible and controversial groups. In the Monroe case, since the Hasidic community had a long history of conflicts with the surrounding communities and the local government, the Supreme Court's decision did not resolve the situation. Similarly, the Oregon case presented a situation that had been divisive for some time and one that directly affected the economic well-being of an entire community. The Oklahoma case falls between these extremes. While there were some previous disputes between the tribe and the state, none that reached the level of conflict in the Monroe or Oregon cases. Moreover, while the Supreme Court case created some legislative reaction, the ultimate response by both parties was compromise rather than ongoing legal and political battles.

The next chapter explores the impact of these decisions, beginning with an examination of the media coverage of these cases, both nationally and locally. This is followed by a comparison of local awareness of these cases with typical national levels of awareness for similar cases. Finally, the chapter explores differences between the immediate and surrounding communities in how strongly the residents felt about the decisions, and how important they perceived the cases to be.

3

Media Attention and Public Awareness

> Most of the Court's decisions do not attract widespread public attention. Most people find it remote and confusing or identify only with its institutional symbols.
>
> – O'Brien (1986, 297)

> Perhaps the best example of the public's ignorance of the Court was a 1989 Washington Post survey. Nine percent correctly named William Rehnquist as Chief Justice of the United States. Among associate justices, recall ranged from 23 percent for Sandra Day O'Connor, to .6 percent for John Paul Stevens. All this pales by comparison with 54 percent who correctly named Joseph Wapner as the judge on the TV show 'The People's Court.'
>
> – Segal and Spaeth (1993, 353)

INTRODUCTION

When the Supreme Court entered into the 2000 presidential election, it placed itself in the middle of one of the most heated political debates in recent memory. While most citizens could probably not explain the subtleties of the legal arguments, virtually everyone knew the decision would ultimately determine the outcome of the election. The reason why the electorate was so well informed is simple: For weeks, the Court's decision was featured in the morning newspaper, on the television evening news, or on the car radio during the morning commute. The Court's decision simply saturated the media, and consequently, people across the nation were interested in the Supreme Court. Many Americans also know of the

Segments of this chapter draw heavily on Hoekstra (2000).

Court's involvement in other controversial issues such as abortion, school desegregation, and flag burning. At other times, such as the nomination hearings for Clarence Thomas or, prior to that, Robert Bork, the Court has also been squarely at the center of American politics.

Even so, most accounts paint a discouraging picture of national public attentiveness to the Supreme Court and its activities. Even among those who read the newspaper on a daily basis and watch the local news or the network's evening news broadcasts, the chances of seeing a story about the Supreme Court on any given day, in any given community, are relatively small. The Court is, to be sure, among the least covered institutions of government (Franklin and Kosaki 1995; Hibbing and Theiss-Morse 1995; Graber 1997). Not only are the justices reluctant to interact with the media, but also the way the Court goes about its business does not readily lend itself to sustained media coverage (Davis 1994; Graber 1997). However, for numerous reasons, some already highlighted in previous chapters, it would be inaccurate to conclude that public interest in the Court is nonexistent. For one thing, perhaps being able to name current justices is not the best indication of how much someone knows about the Court. After all, most Americans cannot recall the names of many members of Congress, including their own representatives.

Another reason why we should be reluctant to conclude that most citizens are ignorant of the Court is that even some research on national levels of awareness questions the assumption that the public is always poorly informed. In a series of studies on the Supreme Court and public opinion in the 1960s and 1970s, Tanenhaus and Murphy (1968a, 1968b; 1981) found that between 40 and 45 percent of a national sample could name at least one Supreme Court decision they either liked or disliked. While they and others have interpreted this to indicate relatively low levels of information, it is important to note that their data were collected immediately following the 1964 and 1966 election cycles – not a time of the year when the Court is at its most active. Moreover, recall reached as high as 80 percent among the better educated respondents. The kinds of cases people could recall were, as expected, ones most likely covered by the media at that time (civil rights, abortion, religion, and the death penalty). Based on these findings, there is good reason to suspect that the public's knowledge of the Court is greater than expected.

More recently, Franklin and his colleagues (Franklin, et al. 1993; Franklin and Kosaki 1995) found evidence of even more widespread knowledge of Court cases; sometimes as high as 40 percent of those interviewed could recall *specific* Court decisions – a rigorous threshold for information about the Court. The reason they uncovered such widespread awareness is simple: They conducted their research with the Court's calendar in mind, and they explicitly evaluated individual characteristics – aside from media coverage – likely to increase attention to cases. Like Franklin and his colleagues, it is important to assess public interest and knowledge when the Court's activities are most salient. Moreover, in such a large and diverse nation, citizens rely on vastly different sources of political information. However, what might be newsworthy in some portions of the country may not be in other parts. Because of the variation in national media coverage of Court decisions, it would be unrealistic and unfair to expect uniformity among members of the mass public. Thus, it is equally important to examine *where* the Court's activities are most visible.

As the stories in the previous chapter suggest, even ordinary cases can generate intense interest to some people, such as members of the local communities where the controversies began. But, no matter how much people want to know about a case, the media must first provide information. Does the media sense this curiosity and cover cases of local concern? If so, does this coverage create an informed local citizenry? Are some people simply more likely to learn about the decision? If so, these patterns are likely to be obscured by looking only at national media coverage and national awareness.

Some of the cases included in this project seem more likely to attract media and public attention than do some of the others. In the upstate town of Monroe, New York, for example, the ongoing tensions between the two communities (Kiryas Joel and the rest of Monroe Township) existed in some form or another for a few decades – ever since the Hasidic community first put down roots in Orange County. The controversy that ultimately winds up on the Supreme Court's docket is merely the latest in that ongoing saga. Over the years, stories about these previous tensions were extensively covered in the local newspaper, *The Times Herald-Record.* While the case might be of lesser interest elsewhere in the nation, there is good reason to suspect that the local media will cover the story and that the local citizenry will have the opportunity to learn about this latest controversy. Those who live outside of the immediate communities of Monroe and Kiryas Joel probably have a less keen interest in the story, but since they live in the same media market, they too should have the opportunity to gain information about the story.

Just as the citizens of Monroe Township might eagerly anticipate the Court's decision regarding the creation of the special school district, so too might the citizens in the logging community of Sweet Home, Oregon, anticipate the Court's decision about the future of the spotted owl. The residents of Sweet Home's surrounding communities would likely be more interested in the Court's decision on this issue than the average citizen living elsewhere with less of a stake in the outcome. Importantly, it should be equally as likely for the local media to provide extensive information about the decision.

The residents of Oklahoma and Center Moriches, New York, should be interested in and attuned to the outcome of the cases from their respective communities. In Oklahoma, the state with the largest population of Native Americans, and specifically in Ada, where the Chickasaws are located, controversies surrounding state and tribal relations occur on a regular basis. Yet, as the stories in the previous chapter suggest, the tensions in the Oklahoma case are simply qualitatively different from the controversies in Monroe and Oregon. In Monroe, previous tensions between the residents of the Villages of Monroe and Kiryas Joel were often settled, if not quite resolved, by separation, rather than accommodation and compromise. In Oklahoma, on the other hand, the evidence suggests that the conflicts between the tribes and the state were usually settled through compromise, even if it took a court battle to instigate that compromise.

Moreover, the disputes in both Oklahoma and Center Moriches did not revolve around an entire community's way of life or livelihood, as was true in both the Monroe and Oregon disputes. The tensions and divisions were simply neither as wide nor as deep as they were in Monroe or in Oregon. In Center Moriches, there was no prior history of tensions between the groups involved, and the Court's decision did not so severely affect the way of life for either of the parties involved. Surely, we can expect they cared about and had a stake in the outcome, but it is unlikely to affect them in the same way or to the same degree as those from Monroe and Sweet Home.

Even though these cases are qualitatively and quantitatively different from one another, all four of the cases should be of significantly greater interest to the local residents than they would be to citizens elsewhere in the country. Each case – either directly or indirectly – affects the local citizens, their neighbors, their elected officials, the local economy, the distribution of tax dollars, or their local schools and school boards. Such is true in virtually every case on the Court's docket. Equally important is that the local media should follow these stories and report back to their communities on new developments in these cases. While each story may show up in the national news, particularly on the day the Court announces its decision, it is less likely that the national media or local media across the nation will focus intensely on the developing controversy, the Court decision, or the aftermath of the decision. There simply would be less immediate or ongoing interest in a case about a controversy in Long Island between a local church and the local high school in the Midwest than on Long Island itself. To be sure, these stories are not exclusively regional stories, and the argument is not purely about geography. The argument is about both *access to* and *interest in* Supreme Court cases. Both of these conditions should be met, to varying degrees, in the local communities where the controversies began.

Consistent with the theme running throughout this book is that reliance on aggregate and national data obscures individual and local patterns. The remainder of this chapter examines how national media coverage and national public attention to Supreme Court activities can mask intense local media coverage and equally intense local citizen interest. The analysis of media attention is both quantitative and qualitative. The quantitative analysis simply examines the number of stories in the papers (both local and national) and on the network news. This serves as the test of the *Media Coverage Hypothesis* which predicts that the local media will pay greater attention to local cases than will the national media. In addition to testing this specific hypothesis, there is also more qualitative analysis looking at how well the local papers convey the nature of the dispute and the Supreme Court's decision.

Next is an examination of how media coverage of Supreme Court cases affects citizens in and around the local community where the controversy began. Specifically, how did local media attention affect local levels of awareness to the four cases included in this study? While the media may have "minimal effects" on people's attitudes toward political issues, they certainly have the power to draw attention to issues and to place them on the political agenda (Iyengar and Kinder 1987; Iyengar 1991). This is exactly what is expected to occur in these local samples. Specifically, recall from Chapter 1 that the *Local/National Awareness Hypothesis* predicts that the intense local media coverage of these cases should produce awareness in these local communities that is much higher than typically found in national samples. Moreover, those from the *immediate* communities should be more interested in these cases than those from the surrounding communities and so they should be more likely to know about the case, just as the *Immediate/Surrounding Awareness Hypothesis* predicts.

Finally, consistent with the research on politically important attitudes, the fact that the case involves people, groups, and officials from the local community, those from the immediate community should rate the issue as more important than those from the surrounding communities (Krosnick, et al. 1993; Boninger, et al. 1995). Thus, the final hypothesis in this chapter is the *Local Importance Hypothesis.*

Each of these hypotheses flows from one another. Media coverage determines the opportunity that citizens have to become acquainted with the information, which in part will determine public attention to the issues. But, as the hypotheses predict, individuals from the different communities are expected to bring different interests to the table, so to speak. Those from the immediate communities are expected to do more with the information than those from the surrounding communities. They should pay greater attention and attach greater interest to the cases than those from the surrounding communities. Moreover, each of these hypotheses has important implications for the topics in the subsequent analysis in Chapter 4, which explores opinion change on the issues, and Chapter 5, which explores change in evaluation of the Court.

DECIDING WHAT TO COVER

While it is true that for much of the year, media coverage of the Court pales in comparison with the elected branches of government, it is also true that coverage of the Court rivals and sometimes even exceeds coverage of the other branches (Franklin and Kosaki 1995; Graber 1997). Coverage peaks when the Court hands down the bulk of its decisions. Although coverage of the Court as an institution may be lacking, coverage of specific decisions, at least on decision day, is not. We also know that the media, at least the national media, are more likely to cover civil liberties and civil rights cases than business and economic cases (Katsh 1983; Slotnick, Segal and Compoli 1994; Slotnick and Segal 1998). Thus, while each of the four cases should generate greater local coverage, there may be differences between the two civil liberty cases and economic cases overall.

There is also some evidence that local coverage might be different. First, Franklin and Kosaki (1995) note this in their examination of media coverage and attention to Supreme Court cases. Their sample was a St. Louis City sample, and, coincidentally, one of their cases originated in St. Louis. While coverage of this case was generally extensive, the coverage in the *St. Louis Post Dispatch* exceeded national coverage. In a series of interviews with newspaper reporters, Richard Davis (1994) notes that regional issues are indeed important to reporters when deciding what cases to cover. Discussing how he chooses which cases to cover, Frank Aukofer of the *Milwaukee Journal* says that he selects "anything that comes out of Wisconsin or Wisconsin courts and occasionally things that are of interest to people in Wisconsin" (Davis 1994, 71). Miranda Spivack of the *Hartford Courant* expresses the same sentiment. She states that her "function is to pick out ten big cases of the year and follow. I will try to get all the Connecticut cases" (Davis 1994, 71).

This is striking evidence. No research systematically examines whether local media are more likely to cover home-grown cases. But it makes sense and suggests additional studies into whether the local media may be doing a better job informing citizens of Court activities than the national media. With this in mind, the next test is that of the *Media Coverage Hypothesis*.

Media Coverage Hypothesis: *The local media should cover local cases more extensively than the national media and the media from other parts of the nation.*

This hypothesis is evaluated using data on local and national media attention to the case both before the Court's decision and once the decision is handed down. Local media attention is measured using coverage in the main local newspaper. National media attention and attention from other parts of the country is measured by looking at coverage in *The New York Times, Los Angeles Times, The Washington Post, St. Louis Post-Dispatch*, and *The Wall Street Journal*. The analysis of media attention of the actual decision also includes coverage on the three networks' evening news broadcasts (ABC, CBS, and NBC). Coverage is measured as a simple count of the number of stories and editorials concerning the cases at the different stages. Coverage of the actual Supreme Court decisions is limited to the two-week period following the announcement of the decision, since the second wave of interviewing typically took place during that same time frame. Network news coverage is counted as the number of seconds in the thirty-minute broadcast on decision day, as well as whether the story led the broadcast.

Media Coverage Prior to the Supreme Court's Decision

The analysis begins with a comparison of local and national coverage at three time periods: while the case was in the lower courts (lower court activity), following the Supreme Court's decision to accept the case (certiorari),[1] and following oral arguments, but before the final decision (oral arguments). This information is included in Table 3-1.

Whether we look at lower court activity, certiorari, or oral arguments, local media coverage of these cases is much more extensive than national media coverage or coverage by local papers in other parts of the nation. As Table 3-1 shows, in each of the four cases, coverage by the local media is always at least twice as large as in any of the other newspapers. Often, it is much more than that. Additionally, differences in coverage *between* the cases are also important to consider. As discussed in Chapter 2, both the Monroe and the Oregon cases captured local and national media interest much more significantly than did either the Center Moriches or the Oklahoma case. This is especially true of the Oklahoma case. Coverage of lower court activity in the Oregon case is particularly noteworthy. In *The Oregonian*, the dominant local newspaper, there were 147 stories. Although national media attention was significantly less, *The New York Times,* for example, included thirty stories.

Many of the stories about the spotted owl were about clashes in the Pacific Northwest between environmentalists and industry more generally. Every article mentioned the role of the courts in resolving the dispute. Often, the story happened to mention the case, but did not focus on it. Still, since these news pieces did mention the lawsuit, they are included in the media coverage analysis. In general, these data on local versus national coverage of the case prior to the Supreme Court's decision strongly support the media coverage hypothesis. This finding is central to the rest of the book. Clearly, residents in and around the communities where the controversies began are much more likely to hear about, and become interested in, the controversy. This should create citizens with more strongly held beliefs; or, at least these residents simply will have given the issues more thought than someone elsewhere in the nation who has not had the same opportunity to learn about the dispute. This finding helps bolster many of the expectations investigated later in the chapter and in the subsequent empirical chapters. Specifically, since this exposure to information should help solidify their beliefs about the issues, they should subsequently: 1) attach greater policy relevance to the issue, 2) be less likely to change their opinion once the Court announces its decision, and 3) be more likely to update their view of the Court based on how they feel about the Court's decision.

---

[1] These stories do not need to be about the certiorari decision per se.

TABLE 3-1. *Media Coverage of the Cases Prior to the Supreme Court's Decision*

	Lower Court Activity	Certiorari	Oral Arguments
	Center Moriches		
Newsday	5	2	1
The New York Times	0	1	0
St. Louis Post-Dispatch	0	2	0
The Wall Street Journal	0	0	0
The Washington Post	0	2	0
Los Angeles Times	1	2	0
	Monroe [a]		
Times Herald-Record [b]	16	15	8
The New York Times	8	5	2
St. Louis Post-Dispatch	1	4	3
The Wall Street Journal	0	0	0
The Washington Post	1	3	1
Los Angeles Times	1	1	2
	Oklahoma		
The Daily Oklahoman	6	3	3
The New York Times	0	0	0
St. Louis Post-Dispatch	0	0	0
The Wall Street Journal	0	0	0
The Washington Post	0	0	0
The Los Angeles Times	0	0	0
	Oregon [c]		
The Oregonian	147	15	11
The New York Times	30	1	0
St. Louis Post-Dispatch	13	0	1
The Wall Street Journal	0	0	0
The Washington Post	23	2	2
Los Angeles Times	27	1	2

[a] The "lower court activity" column in the Monroe case includes a few cases where the Supreme Court issued a stay on July 26, 1993, until the Supreme Court had a chance to decide whether to grant certiorari. Certiorari was eventually granted on November 29, 1993.

[b] In the Monroe case, the entries for the local paper, the *Times Herald-Record*, may be an undercount. This paper does not have a publicly searchable archive, nor is it available on Lexis-Nexis. Instead, the information is based on a list provided by the newspaper's research office. The list is based on a keyword search ("Kiryas Joel" and "school district") and included hundreds of stories. That list only included the date and title of the story. From that scant information, only stories that were clearly about the legal battles were included. Thus, the numbers in the table may underestimate the actual number of stories.

[c] In the Oregon case, many of the stories in the "lower court activity" column are about the Endangered Species Act and court cases in general. Even though many of them do not report on specific court decisions, they do refer to the courts and the general dispute over the spotted owl and the Endangered Species Act. Thus, so long as they mention court involvement, they are counted as covering lower court activity.

Media Coverage Following the Supreme Court's Decision

In addition to differences in the predecisional coverage, there are also differences between national and local coverage of the decision itself. These data are presented in Table 3-2. The Monroe case, involving the school district created for the Hasidic children, received more attention, when measured as the number of minutes on the news or the number of stories in the newspaper, than any of the other cases. It was not, however, the lead story on any of the network's evening news broadcasts. There were two other cases decided on the same day, June 27, 1994, as well as many orders in other cases. One of the other two cases was the First Amendment case about federal regulation of the cable industry. The other was a criminal procedure case. So, there was some competition for media coverage following the decision.

Coverage of the Monroe Decision

Particularly noteworthy is that the number of stories in the local paper, the *Times Herald-Record*, is truly remarkable. In total, there were twenty-five local newspaper stories, one of which was an extended story in the accompanying Sunday magazine. This story was actually written the day before the Court delivered its opinion. Since the end of the term was fast approaching, the reporters and editors must have anticipated that the Court would announce its decision shortly. Considering the ongoing conflicts between the residents of Kiryas Joel and the rest of Monroe Township, this extensive local coverage should not come as a great surprise. This case appeared to be a deeply divisive issue in the general community. During the last decade, there have been numerous stories about the Hasidic community; so, it is not surprising that the Court's decision would receive similarly extensive coverage. Certainly, one thing is clear: the local media covered this case more frequently than did the national media, with seven stories in *The New York Times*, compared with twenty-five stories in the local newspaper. This case proved to be a newsworthy story, both nationally and locally.

Coverage of the Center Moriches Decision

The Center Moriches case was decided on June 7, 1993, along with six other cases: a mortgage case, a banking case, a medicare case, and two criminal procedure cases. So, there was some competition for media coverage. While the dispute between the church and the school board received only scant attention in the national papers – ranging from one to three

TABLE 3-2. *Quantity of Local and National Media Coverage of the Four Cases (including editorials)*

	Center Moriches	Monroe	Oklahoma	Oregon
Local Newspaper Coverage	6 *Newsday*	25 *Times Herald-Record*[a]	2 *Daily Oklahoman* 9 *Ada Evening News*[b]	6 *Oregonian* 2 *Albany Democratic Herald*
Network News[c]				
Time, in Seconds	210	340	0	150[d]
Lead Story on Network	1	0	0	3
National Newspaper Coverage				
The New York Times	2	7	0	4
The St. Louis Post-Dispatch	3	5	0	4
The Wall Street Journal	1	3	0	1
The Washington Post	1	4	0	2
The Los Angeles Times	3	3	0	2

[a] The count of stories in the *Times Herald-Record* includes one story in the Sunday Magazine.

[b] The Oregon decision was handed down the same day as two other cases: a Congressional redistricting case and a religion case. All three cases were reported together on all three networks as the lead story. On all three networks the Oregon case was reported following the other two cases.

[c] Network news coverage refers to the evening news on the day of the decision only.

[d] The number of stories reported here is greater than reported in Hoekstra (2000). The newspaper's research/archive office previously provided the wrong count.

Source: Data for local media coverage of the four cases come from each of the research/archive offices of the newspaper and/or *Academic Universe* (*http://lexis-nexis.com/universe*). Data on television news coverage come from Vanderbilt Television News archives (http://tvnews.vanderbilt.edu/).

stories – the local Long Island newspaper, *Newsday*, covered the decision in a total of six stories – at least twice as many as any of the other papers.

So, consistent with the media coverage hypothesis, the local media devoted more attention than the national media did. Overall, however, this case did not attract nearly as much local attention as did the Monroe case. Considering the differences between these two cases, this is not all that surprising. Unlike the ongoing disputes in Monroe between the members of that community, there was no real history of dissent between the church (Lamb's Chapel) and the residents of the surrounding communities. So, while it is reasonable to expect relatively high coverage in the local community, it is unlikely for the case to receive as much media attention – even by the local media – as did the Monroe case.

Coverage of the Oregon Decision

The case from Sweet Home, Oregon, received local coverage, but not quite as extensively as expected. Like the Center Moriches case, there were six stories in the dominant local paper, *The Oregonian*, and two in the small local paper, *The Albany Democratic Herald*. Given the importance and the salience of the issue to the residents of these communities, it is somewhat surprising that there was not more extensive coverage. As noted in the previous chapter, the dispute between the environmentalists and the logging industry was a top priority to the state and the local communities. Both *The New York Times* and *The St. Louis Post-Dispatch* included four stories about the decision. Other papers ran fewer articles, from one to three. As expected, local media coverage was greater than national exposure or coverage in other parts of the country, but only by a small margin.

One reason for lower national coverage was that there were other decisions handed down the same day, some of which were very salient and newsworthy. One of those cases was *Rosenberger v. Rector and Visitors of University of Virginia*, a highly visible and much anticipated decision on the First Amendment and religion. Another was *Capital Square Review and Advisory Board, et al., v. Pinette*, which also presented a free speech issue. There were also two controversial redistricting cases – one from Georgia and another from Louisiana. With so many high-profile cases, the Oregon case faced tough competition for media attention.

Coverage of the Oklahoma Decision

On the low end of the spectrum is the Oklahoma case, which pitted the state of Oklahoma against the Chickasaw Nation over the collection of motor fuel taxes. Recall from Table 3-1 there was no national coverage of this case prior to the Court's decision either. This case simply did not register with the national media. It was not on any of the three major television networks, nor did any of the national papers cover the decision. Even *The New York Times*, considered to be the nation's "paper of record," did not mention the decision, not even in passing. *The Wall Street Journal*, which prides itself on covering economic issues, also chose to ignore this state taxation controversy. The case faced some competition, with the Supreme Court handing down decisions in four other cases the same day. One case involved federal employment compensation; there was a case about age discrimination in employment, another case presented a double jeopardy question in connection with a drug prosecution; and finally, there was a case about a disability claim.

While the national media did not pay much attention to the Oklahoma case, the local media did. However, considering the large population of Native Americans in Oklahoma as a whole, it is somewhat surprising that there was not greater coverage of this case in the local papers. Perhaps the nature of the issue – gasoline taxes – simply is not as interesting or "newsworthy" as a religious establishment debate – like in the Monroe case. This would be consistent with what other researchers have found, namely, that the media is more likely to cover civil liberty issues than economic ones (Slotnick and Segal 1998). But, this is not a particularly satisfying answer in this instance, when the issue of tribal sovereignty is so central to Oklahoma politics.

A more realistic explanation for the relative lack of media coverage is the timing of the decision. This case was handed down less than two months after the bombing of the Alfred P. Murrah Federal Building in Oklahoma City on April 19, 1995. For obvious reasons, the bombing continued to dominate the local and national news for months. Certainly, two months later the local newspaper had space to run other stories; still, the tragedy remained the predominant story for residents and reporters alike.

Overall Quantity of Local Versus National Coverage

While the Monroe case received the greatest quantity of attention, it was not the lead story on any of the television networks. Obviously, it was an issue of great local interest, but only moderate national interest. Both the Center Moriches case and the Oregon case did lead the news. The Center Moriches case was the lead story on one network, and the decision in the Oregon case was the lead story on all three of the major networks. The Court announced its decision in the Oregon case on the same day as two other, rather dramatic decisions – one involved redistricting and the other a First Amendment religion controversy. The three networks discussed all three decisions within the same story. These two cases, Center Moriches and Oregon, were of some interest nationally, but apparently, they were even more newsworthy locally than nationally. The Oklahoma case appears to be of no interest nationally, and moderate interest locally.

The local papers had at least twice as many stories about the cases than did their national counterparts. The reason for this should be straightforward: The local media have greater incentive to report on issues of local concern. Usually *The New York Times,* for example, will discuss a Supreme Court decision, but the readers of that paper are not likely to have the continued interest in a case from Oregon, as will the people of Oregon. The result is that even sophisticated consumers of the news, those who read *The New York Times*, or any of the other national papers, are less likely to find out about many Supreme Court cases than those who rely on their local papers for information.[2]

In short, there is support for the *Media Coverage Hypothesis*. Although the coverage varies between these four cases, the differences are largely predictable. In general, cases that appear more locally divisive and contentious (i.e., Monroe and Oregon), and those with civil liberties issues (i.e., Center Moriches and Monroe) attracted greater attention both locally and nationally. This finding is important for two reasons. First, although there was some anecdotal evidence from previous research to support the hypothesis, there have been no systematic efforts to examine differences in local versus national media attention to Supreme Court cases. Second, and more critical to the rest of the hypotheses, is that the local communities have an important connection to the cases. It is in these communities where both access and interest are likely to be high enough for the Court's decisions to have an effect on attitudes toward the issues, as well as attitudes toward the Court.

QUALITY OF LOCAL COVERAGE

The previous discussion shows that the local media are more likely to report on Supreme Court cases when the controversy has local roots. However, the sheer volume of coverage is only one aspect to consider. Equally important in creating a well-informed audience is the quality of the coverage. If the local reporters are poorly equipped to understand and accurately convey Supreme Court decisions, as so many others suggest, then all the stories in the world will not be able to increase meaningful knowledge of the Court (Newland 1964; Larson 1985; Davis 1994; Graber 1997). More importantly, the quality of the coverage might mitigate the effect of these decisions. If the local media incorrectly present

---

[2] In order to validate the findings on local versus national coverage using a larger sample of cases, Appendix C presents patterns of media coverage for a sample of twenty-three cases from the Court's 1996–97 term. The data in this appendix show that in about half of the cases, local coverage exceeded coverage in *The New York Times*. In the other half, however, coverage was either equal or more extensive in *The New York Times*. Thus, the four cases are probably not a true random sample of cases from the Court's docket. However, it was also clear that coverage of these cases in the media from other parts of the nation was consistently lower than coverage in the local paper or in *The New York Times*.

the substance of the Court's decisions, it would be unrealistic to expect to uncover systematic changes in people's subsequent feelings about the issues or the Court. Also, the Court would not be able to change individuals' previous attitudes if the media do not attempt to convey much of the reasoning behind the Court's decision.

So, how well do these local papers do? The following pages turn the attention to the quality of both the local and national media coverage. Of primary importance is whether the local media do an adequate job conveying the bottom line of the decision to the local audience. For purposes of comparison, the analysis is conducted on the coverage in the national papers.[3]

Indicators of Quality

Included are four measures of the quality of the coverage. The first is whether the story was written by *staff* reporters (or other staff of the newspaper, including editors). Many accounts of newspaper coverage of the Supreme Court suggest that, other than the large national papers such as *The New York Times* or *The Washington Post*, which assign reporters to the Supreme Court, most papers simply do not have adequate staff to do that. Instead, they must rely on wire services, such as the Associated Press (AP) to deliver the news (Davis 1994). But reliance on AP reports could lower the quality of the coverage since the wire services will not tailor the story for the local audience. It is a much different kind of story than one specifically written for a local audience. Since a wire report must often be out within an hour of the Court's decision, there is little time to analyze the actual opinion, get reactions to the decision, or do much research on the significance of the case.

The second is whether the story adequately conveyed the *background* of the conflict between the two parties involved in the legal dispute. If the story described the background of the conflict, including lower court decisions, how the legislation was created, or other details of the controversy, it was coded as including background coverage. The third indicator is simply whether the story correctly describes the Supreme Court's *decision*. If the story includes what the majority opinion stated, the story is coded positively. It does not need to include the vote, just simply the main holding. For example, if the story said something like, "Yesterday, the Supreme

---

[3] The quality analysis is not done on *The Wall Street Journal* coverage since only abstracts of the stories, not the entire text, are available from Lexis-Nexis.

Court ruled against the creation of the Kiryas Joel school district as a vio-
lation of separation of church and state," it would be coded as accurately
reporting the decision. In other words, if the information was correct and
complete, it was coded positively.

The fourth and final measure of the quality of coverage is whether
the story mentions the existence of any dissenting or concurring opinions
(*separate opinions*). In addition to serving as a good indicator of the quality of coverage, discussion of these separate opinions in the story might
possibly affect reactions to these decisions. The decisions may be less persuasive, and they may affect subsequent evaluations of the Court as well.
The results of the analysis on the quality of coverage are presented in
Table 3-3.

Who Covered the Decision?

So, how often did the local papers resort to wire service reports? Actually, they did not do so very often. The newspaper's staff – usually the
local reporters – wrote the vast majority of the stories. Only *The Ada
Evening News* relied on the AP reports, taking half of their stories on the
gasoline tax case from the wire reports. Of these three AP stories, one
included information on both the background and the decision; another
had information on the decision but not the background; and one had
no meaningful background information, and actually included a factual
error regarding the decision. The staff did a much better reporting job
about this case than the AP did.

There was only one story used by *The Oregonian* editorial staff. The
Times Herald-Record similarly relied on their own staff more than outside
wire services. Only three of the nineteen stories were written by outside
wire services. Instead of the AP, they relied on one story written exclusively
by a reporter from the Ottoway News Service, and two stories were col-
laborations between their own staff and Ottoway News Service reporters.

For the most part, though, each of these local papers covered the stories
using their own staff. As the discussion on the background coverage of
the decisions in the following section shows, they did a good job conveying to their readers the issues involved in the cases. The reports seem to
compensate for whatever lack of legal training they might have with their
knowledge of local issues, events, and participants. They understand the
significance of the events in a way that a wire reporter, a reporter for *The
New York Times,* or a local reporter from some other part of the country
could never understand. A difference emerges in looking at the national
newspapers. More often than not, they rely on their own staff to write

TABLE 3-3. *Quality of Local and National Newspaper Coverage of the Supreme Court's Decisions (excluding editorials)*

	Staff	Background	Decision	Separate Opinions	Newspaper
Center	6/6	3/6	4/6	1/6	*Newsday*
Moriches	2/2	2/2	2/2	1/2	*The New York Times*
	1/1	1/1	1/1	1/1	*The Washington Post*
	1/1	1/1	1/1	1/1	*St. Louis Post-Dispatch*
	3/3	1/3	3/3	1/3	*Los Angeles Times*
Monroe	17.5/19[a]	9/19	17/19	5/19	*Times Herald-Record*
	6/6	3/6	5/6	4/6	*The New York Times*
	2/3	2/3	3/3	1/3	*The Washington Post*
	2/2	1/2	2/2	2/2	*St. Louis Post-Dispatch*
	1/2	2/2	2/2	0/2	*Los Angeles Times*
Oklahoma	2/2	1/2	2/2	–[b]	*The Daily Oklahoman*
	5/8	4/8	5/8	–	*The Ada Evening News*[c]
	0	0	0	–	*The New York Times*
	0	0	0	–	*The Washington Post*
	0	0	0	–	*St. Louis Post-Dispatch*
	0	0	0	–	*Los Angeles Times*
Oregon[d]	5/6	4/6	6/6	1/6	*The Oregonian*
	3/3	1/3	3/3	2/3	*The New York Times*
	1/1	1/1	1/1	1/1	*The Washington Post*
	1/2	1/2	2/2	1/2	*St. Louis Post-Dispatch*
	1/1	1/1	1/1	1/1	*Los Angeles Times*

Note: Cell entries contain the number of stories written by staff, describing the background of the controversy, explaining the Supreme Court's opinion, or mentioning any concurring or dissenting opinions over the number of stories in the newspaper. This table includes only news stories. Editorials and other nontraditional stories are excluded.

[a] The entry of 17.5 for the number of "staff" articles in the *Times Herald Record* is due to a few stories that were coauthored by staff and news service writers.

[b] Since there are no separate opinions on the gasoline tax, these cells were left empty. One story in the Oregonian simply took excerpts from the decision. It is included in the total number of stories (6), but since it was not written by any member of the Oregonian's staff, the total number of staff-written stories is five of six.

[c] The count of Oklahoma stories in *The Ada Evening News* excludes a poll run by the newspaper. Though the poll actually does a good job portraying the background and events, it is hard to code it as a news story.

[d] Hard copies of the two stories written in the *Albany Democrat Herald* are not available. It is a weekly publication that does not provide access to back copies.

these stories, but they also tend to rely on wire services more often than did the local papers. *The New York Times* relied exclusively on its own staff, but each of the other papers used outside services at least once in the coverage of these four cases.

Coverage of the Background

A story that simply states a Court ruling is not nearly as informative as one that conveys the nature of the controversy leading up to the Court case. A history of the legislation in question or lower court decision that created the controversy may engage the reader in a way that a simple description of the Supreme Court's vote and decision simply cannot do on its own. It can show a much larger context than a story about the decision, and can talk about the players involved, and what was at stake in a much more dramatic and meaningful way than can a story simply about the decision. In short, coverage of the background of the case may increase the readers' sense of the importance of the case.

For example, consider the Oklahoma case. At issue, as detailed previously, was the gasoline tax imposed by the state of Oklahoma. A story that simply says, "Yesterday, in the case of *Oklahoma Tax Commission v. Chickasaw Nation*, the Supreme Court unanimously decided that the state of Oklahoma may not impose a tax on the sale of gasoline sold by members of a tribe on tribal land," provides the reader with more information than the just the Court's decision. It also tells the reader the parties involved; but, beyond that, it tells very little about the larger picture. We do not know much about why the state of Oklahoma would want to collect the taxes, why the tax is controversial, or the effect of the tax and the tribe's refusal to pay on other, non-Native American gasoline outlets.

So, how well did these local papers convey the background of these controversies? As Table 3-3 shows, about half of the stories in each of the papers provided background information. So, they missed some opportunities to explain the history of the controversy to their readers. But the data may not tell the whole story. Many of the articles that failed to convey the background information appeared days after the decision and were follow-up pieces about how, for example, the legislatures were responding to the decision. In some of the Oklahoma stories, the story focused on a legislative proposal to change the tax so that the consumer would bear the burden, rather than the seller.

Similarly, in the Monroe case, the focus of a majority of the stories quickly turned toward the state's capital, where the legislature was trying to figure out what to do with the Kiryas Joel School District in light of the recent decision. Again, these stories mentioned the Supreme Court's decision, but did not always convey the background of the controversy. The stories that ran the day after the decisions were most likely to do the best job reporting the background of the controversy. Later stories, on the other hand, quickly shifted their focus to follow the news as it took on new life in the state capital, or back in Washington. Background coverage of the cases and controversies was also spotty in the national newspapers, but may be slightly more likely to appear.

Explaining the Decision

The third indicator of the quality of the coverage is probably the most obvious, and that is how well the newspapers conveyed the central holding in the decision. The story must state what the Court decided and on what grounds it came to that decision. If the story simply said, "Yesterday, the Supreme Court decided that the creation of the special school district for Hasidic children was unconstitutional," that does not accurately explain the reasoning behind the Court's decision. The story must explain the Court's rationale. For example, in the coverage of the Monroe case, a news piece would need to explain that the Court's decision was based on the First Amendment's prohibition against establishment of religion. In the Center Moriches case, the story should mention that the decision was based on the church's free speech rights as guaranteed by the First Amendment. Similarly, in the Oregon case, the story could not simply state that the Supreme Court decided against the logging companies and land owners. Instead, it had to mention that the Court upheld the Secretary of the Interior's interpretation of the Endangered Species Act, or that it upheld regulations protecting the habitat of endangered species, or something reflecting an explanation of the grounds on which the majority opinion based its interpretation. Admittedly, there is more subjectivity in coding the Oklahoma and Oregon cases since it was not possible to simply look for easy catch words like the First Amendment, establishment of religion, separation of church and state, free speech, or free exercise of religion.

On this dimension of quality, the papers did surprisingly well. In the vast majority of cases in both the national and local media, the stories attempted to convey the reasoning behind the Court's decision, and they did so correctly. The one notable exception – and the only real error – was in the one AP account of the gasoline tax case in Oklahoma. That story said that the vote on the gasoline tax was five-to-four, when it was actually unanimous. The Court, however, did divide five-to-four on another issue in the case, the income tax, so the error is understandable. This also supports what others have said about AP stories: in the rush of getting the news on the wire, errors are likely (Davis 1994; Graber 1997). Nearly every other story correctly explains the justification behind the Court's decision.

Typical of how the justification is explained comes from one story in the *Times Herald-Record* two days after the Monroe decision. Local reporters Edward Moltzen and Sylvia Saunders begin their story with the following headline: KIRYAS JOEL BEGINS TOUGH ADJUSTMENT. FEW PREPARED FOR COURT'S DECISION. The first line of the story begins to tell the tale. They write, "No one could say yesterday whether the Kiryas Joel School District even exists any more. The employees came to work. District officials huddled behind the scenes, looking for a new way to teach 200 disabled children from the Village. State lawmakers scurried for a legal solution." Up to this point, they focused on the local impact and also the legislative response. But they quickly began to discuss and explain the actual decision. Beginning in the next paragraph, they write, "The U.S. Supreme Court ruled Monday that Kiryas Joel's School District is unconstitutional." So far, though, they have not conveyed why the Supreme Court decided as it did. That information comes about halfway through the article where they write, "The Supreme Court, in a 6-3 vote, determined the state Legislature's 1989 action creating the Kiryas Joel district in a virtually all-Hasidic community violated the Constitution's establishment clause, separating church and state."

Scholars of the Court might quibble with that description. The Court's opinion had more nuances than the story imparts. But, for the most part, the local reporters conveyed the decision in a way that is typical of the coverage of the other cases. They give the general summary of the decision and its impact on the local community in the first few lines, and then, later in the story, they provide more background, more detail, and simply more information for the interested reader. Certainly, anyone who reads the story has a good understanding of what the Court did. Short of reading actual Supreme Court opinions, law journals, or civil liberties textbooks, this is a reasonable explanation. Anyone who happens to read the story is likely to walk away from that one story with a good understanding of the Court's decision. After all, citizens need not read actual legislation to be considered knowledgeable about Congressional affairs.

Coverage of Separate Opinions
The final indicator of the quality of the local newspaper coverage is whether the stories convey information about separate opinions. Recall from the last chapter that the Center Moriches case was unanimous, but had concurring opinions (written by Scalia and Kennedy). The Court decided the Monroe case by a six-to-three vote and contained both dissenting (Scalia) and concurring (O'Connor) opinions. The Oklahoma case (about

the gasoline tax) was unanimous, and there were no separate opinions on that issue. Finally, in the Oregon case, there was a concurring opinion authored by O'Connor and a dissenting opinion written by Scalia.

Any mention of a separate opinion was coded positively. Although there was a great deal of variance, for the sake of simplicity, any mention of at least one of the separate opinions was coded. This is probably where the local coverage is the weakest. The local papers did not completely ignore the separate opinions, but they also did not spend much time talking about them. In the Monroe case, for example, the separate opinions were mentioned only five times. Some of these were in reference to O'Connor's concurring opinion where she outlined what the state legislature could do to accommodate the Hasidic children without overstepping First Amendment boundaries. Other references were to Scalia's scathing and often sarcastic dissenting opinion. In general, however, the local papers focused on the majority's holding. While they did a good job conveying what the majority ruled, they did not spend that much time discussing the separate opinions.[4] On this account, local coverage does not dramatically differ from national coverage. The national papers included in this analysis also frequently ignored the separate opinions penned by the justices.

Although both the local and national media "fail" to cover the separate opinions, and thus fall short on one dimension of quality, this finding might have important implications. First, the focus on the majority opinion might actually send a more clear signal of the central holding of the case. Had these stories spent more time discussing the concurring and separate opinions, there might be more confusion about the Court's announcement. This clear signal might actually increase the Court's persuasive appeal, the topic of the next chapter, and might also affect subsequent attitudes toward the Court, the core topic of Chapter 6.

Contrary to dire reports on the quality of media coverage, it appears that the regional and local papers do a good job covering many aspects of these cases. They may spend more time discussing the impact of the decision than the decision itself, but this does not indicate "poor quality" coverage. In fact, it is possible they do a better job than some of the national papers who have regular Supreme Court reporters. Such reporters may understand the legal nuances and what the decision means for the

---

[4] This finding is consistent with Hibbing and Theiss-Morse (1995), who argue that one reason for high public support for the Court, at least relative to Congress and the executive, is that the Court is portrayed as a unified institution, and we do not see battles with the Court or between it and other branches. The Court is portrayed as being above partisan "squabbles."

development of legal or constitutional doctrine, but they do not necessarily understand the local issues that led to the cases in the first place. *The New York Times* Supreme Court Correspondent Linda Greenhouse might have a better grasp on the Court's standards for resolving religious establishment than a reporter who works for a relatively small, upstate New York paper. But, in all likelihood, a reporter from Monroe understands the ongoing nature of the conflicts between the Hasidic community and the other residents, or simply knows who Louis Grumet is, or who to call to get an interview. They simply have access to a different set of information.

The local media did their job admirably. But what about the local citizenry? Was all this time and effort wasted? Based on both the quality and quantity of local media coverage, there is a very good chance that the local populace became well informed about these decisions. The next section addresses the question of whether the access to information was enough to peak the interest of the local citizens. It further examines variation between and within the geographic communities.

INFORMED CITIZENS?

Local Versus National Awareness of Supreme Court Cases

This section looks at the impact of the local coverage of these decisions on local levels of awareness of the decisions. Previous analyses showed that the media, to varying degrees, provided an opportunity for the local citizenry to become informed. The question remains as to whether the local citizenry took full advantage of the opportunity. To understand this, the first hypothesis explores differences in local versus national levels of awareness.

Local/National Awareness Hypothesis: Because of the local saturation of media coverage, levels of awareness in these local communities will be higher than typically found in national samples.

Since there was ample opportunity to learn about these decisions, residents in and around these local communities should be better informed than citizens nationally. In order to assess awareness of the cases, the respondents were asked a series of uncued recall questions. To make sure the question did not give the respondents any clues about the decision, the question asked whether they heard anything in the news recently about issue "X," rather than asking whether they heard about recent Supreme

TABLE 3-4. *Awareness of the Supreme Court's Decisions*

Center Moriches	Monroe	Oklahoma	Oregon
82.30%	70.97%	20.69%	40.41%
(113)	(124)	(116)	(146)

Court decision "X" in the news. If they answered affirmatively, they were next asked to describe what they heard. If they mentioned the Supreme Court in their answer, they were asked whether they could recall how the Court decided.

Comparisons of the aggregate levels of awareness, in Table 3-4, show that some of the cases resonated widely. This is particularly true in the Center Moriches case, where an overwhelming majority (82.3 percent) of the entire second-wave sample of respondents knew about the Court's decision; and, in the Monroe case, nearly 71 percent knew about the case. These numbers are astounding given the conventional wisdom that the public knows so little about the Court and its activities. The numbers are even higher than the optimistic results reported previously by Franklin and his colleagues (Franklin, et al. 1993; Franklin and Kosaki 1995). Awareness of the Oregon case was mixed. About 40 percent of the respondents knew about the decision, which is low in comparison to the Center Moriches and Monroe samples; however, it still compares very favorably with national levels. The Oklahoma case, while not totally unnoticed, revealed the lowest levels of awareness – only about 21 percent of the respondents in that sample could recall the Court's decision.

There is definite variation between the samples, which to some extent reflects patterns in the local coverage. The most extensive local coverage was found in the Monroe case, and indeed, knowledge is quite high in Monroe. Local coverage in the other three cases, while higher than the national media coverage, was somewhat lower than the local coverage in Monroe. This partially explains the somewhat lower levels of knowledge in the Oklahoma and Oregon cases. The only deviation is found in the Center Moriches case. Here, knowledge was the highest, yet local coverage came nowhere near the level of coverage in Monroe. But there is certainly evidence that where there is access to information about Court activities, people can and do learn about the Court.

How does local awareness of these cases compare with national levels? While there are no national data on awareness of these particular cases, a comparison can be made with similar cases where national survey data do

TABLE 3-5. *Media Coverage and National Awareness in Franklin, Kosaki, and Kritzer's (1993) Samples*

	Sexual Harassment	Sales Tax	Hate Speech	Tobacco Liability	School Prayer	Abortion
Percent Aware Nationally	0%	15%	24%	30%	28%	40%
Local Newspaper Coverage	10	na	17	7	3	51
National Coverage						
Seconds on Network News	220	380	420	355	395	1,530
Lead Story on Network	1	1	2	1	2	3
The New York Times	1	1	7	6	5	17
St. Louis Post-Dispatch	3	1	3	4	19	42
The Wall Street Journal	1	1	1	5	1	5
The Washington Post	1	1	9	3	12	30
Los Angeles Times	1	2	3	4	8	28

Note: The local newspapers are: *Atlanta Journal Constitution* (sexual harassment), *St. Paul Pioneer Press* (hate speech), *The Record* (tobacco liability), *The Providence Journal Bulletin* (school prayer), and *The Harrisburg Patriot* (abortion). Network news coverage refers to the evening news on the day of the decision only. Newspaper coverage includes editorials. The tobacco and school prayer decisions were handed down on the same day. The Vanderbilt transcripts of the coverage of these two cases on CBS listed them under one subheading. That listing stated that the combined coverage lasted four minutes, ten seconds. This number is divided in half so that each is listed as having been discussed for two minutes, five seconds (125 seconds each). The percentage who were aware probably overestimates the level of awareness since it is the high point of awareness in Franklin, Kosaki and Kritzer's study. The percentage aware is total awareness during the entire two-week period. In short, the comparison between the four cases included in this study and Franklin, Kosaki, and Kritzer's is a conservative comparison.

Source: Data on the local newspaper coverage for Franklin, Kosaki, and Kritzer's cases were obtained from *Online Resources*, a fee-based newspaper archive or from Lexis-Nexis. Data on television news coverage come from Vanderbilt Television News archives (*http://tvnews.vanderbilt.edu/*).

exist. The best comparable data come from Franklin, Kosaki, and Kritzer (1993), who assess national awareness of six cases from the Court's 1991–92 term. This information is presented in Table 3-5, along with relevant media information for their set of cases. In their study, they examine national levels of awareness for a sexual harassment case (*Franklin v. Gwinnett County Public Schools*), a sales tax case (*Quill Corp. v. North Dakota*), a hate speech case (*R.A.V. v. City of St. Paul*), a tobacco company liability case (*Cipollone v. Liggett Group*), a school prayer case (*Lee v. Weisman*), and an abortion case (*Planned Parenthood of Southeastern Pennsylvania v. Casey*). As the data in the table show, national levels of awareness for Franklin, Kosaki, and Kritzer's cases range from a low of virtually no awareness nationally (the sexual harassment case) to a high of 40 percent nationally (the abortion case).[5]

In both the Center Moriches and Monroe samples, awareness exceeds national levels of awareness in the most similar cases in Franklin, Kosaki, and Kritzer's (1993) study. For example, in a comparison between the Center Moriches case – which was discussed in six local newspaper stories and two *New York Times* stories – and the tobacco liability case – which was covered in seven local news stories and six *New York Times* stories – local levels of awareness were much higher, more than two times as high. In fact, awareness in both the Center Moriches and Monroe samples exceeds even the abortion decision included in the 1993 study. In Oregon, too, local levels of awareness are higher than national levels of awareness for any of the similar cases. That case even has a slight advantage over national levels of awareness of the abortion decision, which flooded the national news.

Only in the Oklahoma sample are local levels of awareness similar to national levels. Approximately 20 percent of the Oklahoma sample knew about the Supreme Court's decision on the state gasoline tax. This is higher than national levels of awareness of the sexual harassment and sales tax case in Franklin, Kosaki, and Kritzer data, but less than for their other cases.[6] Again, it is important to note that one reason for the relatively low

---

[5] This table reports the highest level of awareness in their national samples. Their study also reports awareness for each day following the Court's decision. There is a definite peak at the time of the decision followed by a gradual decline. The measure reported for the four studies included in this book is total awareness throughout the sampling period, regardless of the amount of time lapsed between the decision and the survey. This provides for a conservative comparison between their study and the results presented here. The abortion decision is a bit of an outlier in terms of media attention. It appears in seventeen *New York Times* articles, and the three major networks made it the lead story on the evening news broadcast, devoting a combined 1,530 seconds of air time to the decision. Their sexual harassment decision is also somewhat of an outlier. It received moderate attention in the national media, yet it did not register with the national public at all.

[6] Since the four cases included in this project and two of Franklin, Kosaki, and Kritzer cases specifically mention the city or school board in the name of the case, one other media comparison is made for the sake of caution. This comparison is based on a random sample of cases from the Court's 1996–97 term and examines local and national media coverage of those cases. These data are included in Appendix C. Although there are no corresponding data on national levels of awareness of these cases, the findings generally support the findings regarding local media coverage. Approximately half the cases from the 1996–97 term received greater local than national media attention. Since about half of the cases are similar to the four cases on this dimension, it is impossible to claim that the four cases are clearly a random sample of cases from the Court's docket. However, for

levels of media, and hence public attention to the case in Oklahoma, may result from the other extraordinary events surrounding the bombing of the federal building in Oklahoma City. Although it is only speculation, it would be safe to guess that knowledge about the case would have likely been higher had the tragedy not happened.

This analysis, while not perfectly comparable, provides strong evidence that the local media's tendency to cover local cases has an enormous impact on awareness. Citizens of the local communities are much more likely to hear about home-grown Court cases than is typically found in national surveys. The reason for this is equally clear: They simply have greater access to information. One would expect similarly high levels of awareness in the local communities, as opposed to national samples, in Franklin, Kosaki, and Kritzer's cases. Local media coverage of their cases actually exceeds local coverage of the four cases selected in this book. It should not be surprising, then, if local awareness of their cases met, or exceeded, the levels of these four cases.

Awareness in Immediate versus Surrounding Communities

The next section tests the other hypothesis regarding awareness of the Court's decisions.

Immediate/Surrounding Awareness Hypothesis: Levels of awareness among residents in the immediate communities will be higher than among residents of the surrounding communities.

Is there any reason to expect differences *within* each of the four samples? Residents in the immediate and surrounding communities have roughly equal access to information about these cases, but are they equally interested in this news? It is reasonable to expect those who reside in the immediate communities to pay greater attention to the cases than those from the surrounding communities. Though the local media provided roughly similar access to information, those from the immediate community should have greater motivation to seek it out.

those cases with local media coverage equal to or less extensive than national attention (i.e., *The New York Times*), there was even less, if any, coverage elsewhere in the nation. In other words, cases were covered by the local media, and *The New York Times*, but not by the local media in other parts of the country. This supports the claim that the local media are important in disseminating information about the Supreme Court, even if the four cases are not a true random sample of cases from the Court's docket.

TABLE 3-6. *Aggregate Levels of Awareness of the Supreme Court's Decision by Geographic Proximity*

	Immediate Community	Surrounding Community
Center Moriches	85.1%	78.3%
N	(67)	(46)
Monroe	74.1%	68.6%
N	(54)	(70)
Oklahoma[a]	39.0%	10.7%
N	(41)	(75)
Oklahoma (second wave only)	35.0%	13.6%
N	(20)	(22)
Oregon[a]	47.3%	33.3%
N	(74)	(72)
Oregon (second-wave only)	56.3%	42.9%
N	(16)	(14)
Pooled[a]	62.7%	44.1%
N	(236)	(263)

Note: The number in parentheses is the number of respondents successfully contacted who agreed to participate in the second wave.

[a] The difference between the immediate communities and the surrounding communities is significantly different at $p < .05$.

The reasoning is that the more important the issue is to an individual, the greater the motivation to pay attention and spend time thinking about it and its political implications (Petty and Cacioppo 1986; Fiske and Taylor 1992; Krosnick, et al. 1993). The perception of importance does not need to come from material self-interest. It has multiple sources. In fact, social psychologists emphasize the subjective sense of importance (Boninger, et al. 1995). Other sources of importance may include such considerations as identifying with the people involved, such as members or groups from one's local community (Boninger, et al. 1995). This suggests that those from the immediate community may have more information about the case than those from the surrounding communities. Table 3-6 presents the data testing this hypothesis.

In Table 3-6, the awareness results are disaggregated by whether the respondents reside in the immediate community or in the surrounding towns and communities. Also included are reports of awareness among those who were only sampled following the decision (the second-wave only samples). Recall from Chapter 1 that additional samples were created in two studies (Oklahoma and Oregon) in order assess whether

participation in the first wave of the study increased awareness and attention to the case among those included in both waves above and beyond what would have happened naturally. In each of the four samples,
as well as in the second-wave-only samples, awareness in the immediate
community is indeed higher than in the surrounding communities. This
suggests that beyond access to information, living in the immediate community triggers a sense of identification with the parties, or at least a
greater interest in the case. However, these data are certainly not conclu-
sive. Since this is not a true experiment, where individuals are randomly
assigned to residence in the local or surrounding communities, other explanations for this observed pattern might exist. Specifically, the decision
to live in Monroe Township, as opposed to the surrounding communities
in Orange County, might be driven by other factors – factors that might
also be related to interest and knowledge in this case. The effect of local
residence might be determined more conclusively by looking at whether
this pattern holds after controlling for individual level characteristics,
such as attention to media, frequency of engaging in political discussions,
level of education, and gender, each of which increases political knowledge in general, and knowledge of Supreme Court activities in particular
(Franklin and Kosaki 1995). In addition, Franklin and Kosaki (1995)
show that case-specific factors, such as religion and race, may increase
awareness of cases that deal with those issues. For example, Catholics
should be more likely to pay attention to abortion decisions, and African
Americans should pay more attention to discrimination cases. Similarly,
those from the immediate community should pay greater attention than
those from the surrounding communities.

To test for the effect of geographic proximity on attention to Court
cases, the analysis looks at the effect of town of residence, while controlling for factors previously shown to influence awareness of Court
decisions. The dependent variable is simply whether the respondent knew
how the Court decided. It is a dichotomous variable: 1 indicates that the
respondent knew about the decision, 0 otherwise. Because the dependent
variable is dichotomous, the relationship is analyzed using a logit model.
Included in the analysis are measures of attention to media and politics,
education, gender, and geographic proximity.

Attention to politics and media are measured as the number of days
in the last week the respondent had (1) watched the news on television
(*Television Viewing*), (2) read the news in a daily newspaper (*Newspaper
Reading*), and/or (3) discussed politics with others (*Political Discussion*).
The question for each of these measures is similar. Specifically, respondents
were asked "How many days in the last week did you . . ." Thus, responses

TABLE 3-7. *Factors Increasing the Probability of Hearing about the Supreme Court's Decision (Logit Analysis)*

	Center Moriches	Monroe	Oklahoma	Oregon
Town of Residence	.43	.65	1.98**	.98**
	(.55)	(.46)	(.59)	(.41)
Gender	−.56	1.08**	1.62**	.68*
	(.59)	(.47)	(.62)	(.38)
Newspaper Reading	.19*	.13	.26**	.05
	(.10)	(.09)	(.12)	(.06)
Television Viewing	.13	−.22*	.04	.00
	(.10)	(.10)	(.12)	(.08)
Political Discussions	–	.15	.19*	.25**
		(.11)	(.11)	(.08)
Education	.63**	.39*	.21	.18
	(.28)	(.21)	(.25)	(.18)
Constant	−1.63	−.84	−5.86**	−2.37**
	(1.04)	(.86)	(1.33)	(.77)
N	112	122	115	145
−2* Log Likelihood Ratio	88.41	128.65	85.08	174.59
% Correctly Predicted	83.93	76.23	82.61	68.28
1 =	83.04	70.49	20.87	40.69
0 =	16.96	29.51	79.13	59.31

Note: The measure of the frequency of political discussions with friends or neighbors was not included in the Center Moriches study. $*p < .05$ $**p < .01$, one-tailed hypothesis test. Standard errors are in parentheses.

range from 0 to 7, representing the number of days they had engaged in the previous activities. Each is from the second wave. *Education* is measured on a five-point Likert scale that ranges from 1 (less than high school) to 5 (post-graduate education). *Gender* is coded male (1) and female (0). *Town of residence* is coded 1 for those who reside in the immediate community, 0 for those who reside in the surrounding area (see Appendix B for question wording). Each variable should positively affect the probability of learning about the specific Court decision. Table 3-7 presents the results.

The results from this analysis revealed that in two of the four studies (Oklahoma and Oregon), living in the immediate community increased the probability of hearing about the Court's decision. Only in Center Moriches and Monroe, where there were very high levels of awareness and little aggregate variation between the local community and surrounding areas, did *town of residence* prove statistically insignificant; yet, in both cases the variable was in the predicted direction. As expected, *gender, education,* and the frequency of *newspaper reading* and *political discussions* were also important explanations of individual levels of awareness. Unexpected was the null effect of *television viewing*. Previous research suggests that Americans get most of their news from television (Graber 1997; Slotnick and Segal 1998). Here, greater attention to television did not seem to increase one's knowledge of the Court's activities. Without data on the local television news broadcasts, it is difficult to say why this was the case.

These results reinforce the previous findings that 1) access to media information is important, and 2) individual factors also play a crucial role. One of those key factors appeared to be, in at least two of the cases, geographic proximity to the issue. In the other two cases, however, the other variables measuring individual differences cancelled the effect of *town of residence*. In short, there was mixed support for the effect of local proximity on increased awareness.

In order to better understand the substantive effect of *town of residence* along with the other independent variables, Table 3-8 includes predicted probabilities. The probabilities are arranged according to level of *education*, attention to the media (*newspaper reading* and *television viewing*), and the frequency of engaging in *political discussions*. Residents from the immediate and surrounding communities are analyzed separately. Overall, the probability of having heard of the Court's decision increases with *education* and with attention to politics. More importantly for the purposes of this study, people from the immediate community are more likely to hear about the decision than those from the surrounding communities.

The data in Tables 3-7 and 3-8 are consistent with what we know about the effect of education, gender, and engagement in politics on levels of political knowledge. What is more important is that the data reveal how one measure of interest – geographic proximity to the origins of a controversy – might increase attention to and interest in a specific Supreme Court case, even after controlling for the other variables. The effect is statistically significant in two of the four cases – Oklahoma and Oregon. In the other two cases, Monroe and Center Moriches, residents of the immediate and surrounding communities are equally likely to have heard of the decision. In Monroe, this might simply be because there was such intense media coverage in the dominant local newspaper that even those who reside elsewhere, who were only moderately interested in the case, could not help but hear or read about the decision. The finding, or lack thereof, between the two geographic samples in the Center Moriches study is more difficult to explain. It is possible that the case did not trigger any

TABLE 3-8. *Predicted Probabilities of Having Heard about the Supreme Court's Decision*

	Male Education = 1 Newspaper Reading = 1 Television Viewing = 1 Political Discussions = 1	Male Education = 3 Newspaper Reading = 4 Television Viewing = 4 Political Discussions = 4	Male Education = 3 Newspaper Reading = 7 Television Viewing = 7 Political Discussions = 7
Center Moriches			
Immediate	.31	.80	.91
Surrounding	.22	.72	.87
Monroe			
Immediate	.83	.92	.94
Surrounding	.72	.86	.88
Oklahoma			
Immediate	.17	.58	.86
Surrounding	.03	.16	.46
Oregon			
Immediate	.44	.74	.87
Surrounding	.23	.51	.72

greater interest among Center Moriches residents than it did for those from the surrounding communities. While incredibly high, interest in the case may simply be equal for both groups. Given the low salience of the church group to local politics, this makes sense. As the discussion in the previous chapter suggests, Lamb's Chapel was not a salient group in the community. What's more surprising then is the overall high levels of attention to this case given that lack of previous salience.

The statistically significant differences in the Oklahoma case and the Oregon case may also be caused by another factor. In both of these studies, the dominant local paper covered both the immediate community and surrounding community samples. However, in each case there was a smaller newspaper operating in the immediate communities. In the Oregon case, for example, one of the local papers, the *Albany Democrat-Herald*, is published in Albany, a nearby community, and circulates in the immediate community of Sweet Home, and a few of the surrounding communities. But, its circulation does not reach all of those who were sampled as part of the surrounding communities sample, namely the Portland area. Similarly, in Ada, there is a small local paper, *The Ada Evening News*, that circulates in the immediate community, but not in the surrounding communities. However, virtually none of the respondents who knew of the Court decision cited either of those as their primary source of information. So, while not likely to cause a spurious effect, this possibility cannot be completely eliminated either.

THE LOCAL IMPORTANCE OF THE ISSUE

This chapter's final hypothesis explores whether the residents of the immediate community are more likely to perceive the issue as important than are their counterparts who reside in the surrounding towns and communities. Specifically the hypothesis states,

Local Importance Hypothesis: Those from the immediate community should perceive the case as more important than those from the surrounding communities.

The survey instrument included four measures of perceptions of importance in both waves of the survey: 1) how strongly the individual felt about the issue (*Strength of Opinion*), 2) how much time they spent thinking about the issue (*Time Thinking*), 3) how important the issue was to them personally (*Personally Important*), and 4) how important it was to their community (*Important to Community*). Specifically, the survey asked respondents about their opinions on the issue followed by a question asking them "how strongly do you feel about this issue?" Respondents were then asked the following three questions: "Compared to other issues you might think about, 1) how much time do you spend thinking about this issue?, 2) how important is this issue to you personally?, and 3) how important is this issue to your community? Each of these indicators is measured on a three-point scale from 1 (not very strongly/often/important) to 3 (very strongly/often/important). Unfortunately, the Center Moriches survey only included a single measure of importance (*Strength of Opinion*). A summary measure (*Summary*) was created and reported as well. This measure is simply an additive measure of the responses to each of these four items. It ranges from 0 to 12. Of greatest interest are the respondents' perceptions of the importance of the issue after hearing the Court's decision. Thus, Table 3-9 presents those second-wave ratings of importance.

In each study, there is some evidence that the members of the geographic communities rate the importance of the issues in the cases differently. In the Center Moriches study, which included only the measure of how strongly the respondents felt about the issue, the residents of the

TABLE 3-9. Perceptions of Importance in the Geographic Communities

	Center Moriches		Monroe		Oklahoma		Oregon	
	Immediate	Surrounding	Immediate	Surrounding	Immediate	Surrounding	Immediate	Surrounding
Strength of Opinion	2.24 (.10)	2.53 (.12)	2.48 (.10)	2.39 (.11)	2.50 (.16)	1.87 (.23)	2.66 (.10)	2.50 (.11)
$p <$	.03		.29		.02		.15	
N	53	34	40	46	16	8	34	24
Time Thinking	—	—	1.87 (.13)	1.79 (.09)	1.81 (.16)	1.37 (.18)	2.29 (.12)	2.29 (.17)
$p <$			.31		.06		.50	
N			39	48	16	8	34	24
Personally Important	—	—	2.10 (.11)	2.00 (.11)	2.25 (.17)	1.50 (.19)	2.35 (.13)	2.25 (.12)
$p <$			.26		.01		.29	
N			40	48	16	84	34	24
Importance to Community	—	—	2.80 (.08)	2.31 (.11)	2.75 (.14)	2.25 (.25)	2.85 (.09)	2.38 (.15)
$p <$			.00		.04		.00	
N			39	45	16	8	34	24
Summary	—	—	9.26 (.27)	8.63 (.32)	9.31 (.47)	7.00 (.42)	10.13 (.26)	9.50 (.45)
$p <$			.07		.00		.10	
N	53	34	39	43	16	8	32	22

Note: Analysis restricted to those who were aware of the decision. Cell entries are means. Standard errors in parentheses. Probabilities are based on one-tailed difference in means test. The summary measure is combination of all four of the importance ratings.

surrounding communities, not the residents of the immediate community, reported feeling more strongly about the issue. It is possible that this is not the best measure of importance since it also fares poorly in the Monroe and Oregon studies. However, recall that the residents of the immediate community also were not more likely to pay greater attention to this case than were the residents from the surrounding communities. These two findings suggest that at least in this case, the distinction between the immediate and surrounding communities may not be all that important, contrary to expectations.

In the remaining three studies, the evidence is generally as expected. Those from the immediate communities rated the issues as more important than did their counterparts in the surrounding communities. In all three studies that included the measure, those from the immediate community rated the issue as more important to the local community than did those from the surrounding communities. In the Oklahoma study, all of the measures of importance are rated higher than those from the surrounding communities. In all, two items produced the most consistent results: assessing respondents' perceptions of the *importance to community*, and the *summary* measure.

In short, there is moderately strong evidence to support the hypothesis. This is important for two reasons: 1) It suggests that members of the public perceive some Court decisions as more important than others, and that this is due to more than mere exposure to the information. People from both communities had roughly equal access to the information, yet those from the immediate community often perceived the issue as more important to the community. 2) This finding is the underlying assumption of the hypotheses tested in the following chapters.

CONCLUSION

This chapter focused on the first-order public reaction to Court decisions: media attention, citizen awareness, and citizen interest. The results show that while the national media may not pay close, careful, or sustained attention to many Supreme Court cases, the local media often does. This was true before the case ended up on the Court's docket, as well as after the Court handed down its decision. Since these cases involved local officials and local citizens, members of the local media found the case more newsworthy than cases that originated elsewhere. However, there was a wide variance between the cases. To a large extent, this variance can be accounted for by the nature of the dispute. Cases with a previous history, as chronicled in the preceding chapter, and those with a civil liberty dimension, received greater attention. The local media also did a reasonable job explaining the background and decisions to their consumers. The result is that not only do local citizens have greater access to information to these cases, but they are also interested and pay attention. This extensive and careful local coverage led to local levels of awareness exceeding national levels of awareness, often by huge margins. This was particularly true when the case came from the immediate community rather than a surrounding community, but this was not consistently so.

While the results were mixed, residents from the immediate community were more likely to perceive the case as important than were those from the surrounding communities. This implication is important for a number of reasons. First, it suggests that when pople learn about Court cases – and some mechanism triggers an identification with the individuals or issues in the case (here geography) – they are more likely to seek out information and to feel strongly about the issues. Second, it may mean that residents of the immediate communities will be harder to persuade that the decision is the right one. Since local officials will often be crucial to successful implementation of these decisions, they may be less willing to do so than if the Court could persuade the local residents. Third, those who feel strongly about an issue in a case may be more likely to express dissatisfaction with the Court following an unpopular decision. The following two chapters turn to these implications in greater detail.

Chapter 4 turns its attention to one of these second-order effects: whether the Court is able to increase support for the position it takes in its decisions; and, if so, whether this is contingent on other variables, such as support for the Court and geographic proximity. These other variables include individual level support for the Court and geographic proximity. Since research on political attitudes suggests that individuals with more strongly held beliefs are less susceptible to persuasion, those from the immediate community should be less likely to change their opinions. Furthermore, as explored in Chapter 5, those with more strongly held beliefs should be more likely to use this information to update their evaluation of the Court. If these hypotheses hold true, they present the Court with a possibly troublesome dilemma. The local communities where the Court's decisions need to be implemented are the very communities where this task could prove most difficult, and where, as a result, the Court risks its popularity.

At the very least, the results from this chapter challenge previous research portraying the public as uninformed of all but the most salient and controversial Court decisions. Here, the questions are about how geographic proximity increases media attention, and hence, public awareness. Yet, these effects can occur wherever and whenever other media pay attention. As long as citizens are interested in an issue and learn about the Court's actions, it is realistic to expect higher levels of awareness and interest than previously believed possible. Further research needs to identify other situations where these conditions might exist.

4

Changing Hearts and Minds?

Examining the Legitimation Hypothesis

> The Court cannot buy support for its decisions by spending money and, except to a minor degree, it cannot independently coerce obedience to its decrees. The Court's power lies, rather, in its legitimacy, a product of substance and perception that shows itself in the people's acceptance of the Judiciary as fit to determine what the Nation's law means and to declare what it demands.
>
> – Justice Sandra Day O'Connor[1]

INTRODUCTION

Knowledge of a Court case is a prerequisite for it to have an effect on public opinion; but, the apparent lack of public awareness has been the single most difficult obstacle in real-world studies of the Court's persuasive appeal. However, the previous chapter revealed that extensive local media coverage of these four local cases resulted in intense public interest and knowledge of the cases. While there were differences between these cases, in general, there was substantial support for the hypotheses about media attention, public awareness, and perceptions of importance.

Coverage of the Monroe case was incredibly extensive and produced high levels of awareness across both geographic samples. In the Center Moriches case, media coverage was moderately high, certainly higher than national media interest, and this local coverage produced the highest levels of awareness across all four cases. As with the Monroe case, knowledge was nearly equal between the samples, especially after

---

[1] *Planned Parenthood of Southeastern Pennsylvania v. Casey* (1992).

controlling for other factors, such as interest in politics and level of education.

In the Oregon spotted owl case, media coverage was also high, especially compared with national coverage. Public attention was moderately high – higher than we would expect nationally – but there were differences between the various geographic communities. Consistent with expectations, those from the immediate community were more knowledgeable about the case than were those from the surrounding communities, even after controls for the usual suspects were included in the analysis. Media attention and levels of awareness were lowest in the Oklahoma gasoline tax case. However, as with the Oregon case, knowledge was higher in the immediate community – the community where the controversy emerged – than it was in the surrounding communities.

Finally, in the previous chapter, there was evidence – albeit mixed – that those from the immediate community rated the issues in the cases as more important than those from the surrounding communities. This finding was most robust when respondents were asked how important they felt the issue was to their community. In all three studies where the measure was included (Monroe, Oklahoma, and Oregon), the residents of the immediate community thought the issue was more important to their community than did their counterparts in the surrounding communities. This finding is critical for the topics investigated in this chapter as well as the following chapter.

The focus of inquiry in this chapter is the effect of these decisions on the local residents' attitudes on the issues. The high levels of media attention, public awareness, and perceptions of importance hold open the possibility that these Court decisions may affect citizens' feelings about the issue in question. Specifically, the results from this chapter are intended to answer the question of whether the Court's ruling in support of the church increased local support for allowing the church access to the high school auditorium in Center Moriches. What about in Monroe? Did the Court's decision overturning the specially created school district for the Hasidic children change attitudes about the creation and existence of the school district? What about the Court's decision against Oklahoma's levying of gasoline tax against the Chickasaws? Or, the decision to protect the habitat of the spotted owl in Oregon?

If the Court can indeed influence public opinion, it can have a huge impact on the course of public policy. The ability to change public opinion on issues can, over time, lead to sweeping changes in the kinds of policies elected officials choose to pursue. At the very least, increased support for the Court's position would improve the incentives for local officials to enforce the Court's decision (Johnson and Canon 1998). On the other hand, if the Court has little or no effect on public opinion, then it may face hostility, resistance, or outright defiance from these same officials. This question is of great consequence for the Court, especially since members of these local communities seem very knowledgeable about these Court decisions.

To understand whether the Court can influence public opinion, it is first necessary to look for aggregate shifts in support for the issues across all respondents. Although such a simplified form of persuasion is not expected, it is the first step in building a model that more accurately reflects the complexity of the process. After looking for any overall patterns, the next task is to look at attitude change as a function of geographic proximity to the case and also as a function of prior support for the Court, first by examining the bivariate relationships and then by building multivariate models. Finally, the chapter considers how exposure to political information and education affect the persuasion process. But first, there is a review of the most relevant research on public reaction to Supreme Court decisions in order to better elaborate and justify the specific hypotheses developed and tested below.

THE SUPREME COURT AND THE DYNAMICS OF PUBLIC OPINION

The Supreme Court often finds itself in the midst of intense political battles. In recent decades, it has been asked to end legally sanctioned discrimination based on race and gender, to provide access to abortion in the fifty states, to consider the constitutionality of capital punishment, and most recently, to determine the outcome of a hotly disputed presidential election. In many popular and scholarly accounts, the Court's decisions in these areas have changed both public policy and public opinion (Hochschild 1984; Franklin and Kosaki 1989; Johnson and Martin 1998; Canon and Johnson 1998). But there is far from any consensus on whether these changes have in fact materialized, whether they have created support or opposition for its policies, and even in those instances where positive change is found, whether it can be fairly and properly attributed to the Court's actions (Marshall 1988, 1989; Rosenberg 1991).

The most frequently cited account of the Court's legitimacy conferring abilities is the work of Dahl (1957) discussed in Chapter 1. Dahl's seminal work suggests that while the Court is rarely out of step with the dominant lawmaking majorities because of the relative frequency of the appointment process, its main function is to lend its legitimacy to

the policies it upholds. Though Dahl's main interest was the countermajoritarian question – whether the Court actually decides cases contrary
to public opinion – the assumption underlying his conclusion is that the
Court can generate greater acceptance for the policies created in other
branches of government. In short, his work assumes that Court decisions
are powerful – they can cast legitimacy on public policy and can shape
public attitudes on even the most controversial issues.

On the other hand, scholars such as Rosenberg (1991) are more skeptical about the Court's ability to bring about social change. In his com-
prehensive examination of changes in public policy and public attention
toward desegregation, criminal justice, reapportionment, and abortion, he
finds that Court decisions were rarely instrumental in affecting changes.
Instead, any changes that materialized in the wake of Court decisions were
more likely the result of actions taken by other political leaders, changing
market conditions, or trends that predated the Court's actions.

Rosenberg's conclusions proved unsettling to many scholars of the
Court. For one thing, as Caldeira (1991) notes, scholars steadfastly believe
that the Court can and does protect minority rights. Thus, his findings
struck a chord. His research also generated many empirical debates. Most
notably, Canon and Johnson (1998) argue that Rosenberg underestimates
the Court's impact on issues such as abortion and desegregation, and even
on issues that require implementation by other government actors (e.g.,
reapportionment). They also argue that Rosenberg's analysis omits certain important issues such as religion in schools and the availability of
sexually oriented material. These issues, they argue, are prime examples
of the Court's effectiveness in producing important social change. Regardless of their differences in their interpretation of the Court's actual effect,
both Rosenberg (1991) and Canon and Johnson (1998) recognize that
many policies require the willing implementation of other political and
legal actors. Although public opinion was not the central focus of either
of these works, both suggest that the Court's ability to increase public
support for its decisions would increase the willingness of other actors to
implement faithfully. This argument makes a great deal of sense. Since
many political actors serve at the will of the people, it is in their best
interest to serve those constituents.

However, in one of the most exhaustive empirical examinations of
changes in public opinion in the wake of Court decisions, Marshall (1988,
1989) finds little to no evidence of shifts in public opinion. In fact the
average opinion shift was less than 1 percent. In instances where there
was an observable shift, opinion was just as likely to shift against the

direction of the Court's decision. Other research on the effect of public opinion finds more evidence of change, but that the patterns can be more complex than simple shifts in the direction of the Court's decision. Franklin and Kosaki (1989), for example, find that attitudes toward abortion changed following the Court's 1973 decision in *Roe v. Wade*. However, instead of an aggregate shift more favorable toward easier access to abortion, they find a more complicated pattern. In the less controversial dimensions of abortion policy (i.e., rape, medical complications) there was a positive shift in favor of increased access. But for the more controversial area of discretionary abortions, they discovered that those who were initially supportive of access to discretionary abortions became increasingly supportive while those who were initially opposed became even more so. In the aggregate it appeared as if there were no changes in public opinion, but when broken down into how people felt about the issue initially, important changes emerged. Thus, as discussed in Chapter 1, reliance on aggregate data may hide interesting individual level patterns.

Johnson and Martin (1998) discover similar empirical patterns in their examination of public opinion on the issue of capital punishment. They caution that these results are obtained only when the Court makes an *initial* ruling on a *controversial* issue. According to their argument, when the Court hands down subsequent decisions, citizens' attitudes will be fairly well established. Both Franklin and Kosaki (1989) and Johnson and Martin (1998) attribute these findings to the highly charged nature of the cases. Court decisions on more mundane issues, ones that people may not have attended to so thoroughly, should not produce the same patterns of polarization.

There is no consistent finding regarding the effect of Court decisions on public opinion. Further complicating matters are the results from experimental research. In the controlled environment of an experimental lab, researchers have been more successful in finding consistent and robust patterns of persuasion in response to Court decisions (Mondak 1991; Hoekstra 1995; but see Bass and Thomas 1984). This research typically finds that under certain conditions and for specific issues, the Court can increase support for its decisions.

One reason why experimental research may uncover different results from those found by Franklin and Kosaki (1989) and Johnson and Martin (1996) may be the nature of the issues. Franklin and Kosaki (1989) and Johnson and Martin (1996) look at attitudes toward abortion and capital punishment, while experimental research usually looks at less charged issues such as property rights, sexually explicit material, police searches, and censorship of high school newspapers, to name just a few. This, in fact, is exactly the explanation offered by both Franklin and Kosaki (1989) and Johnson and Martin (1996). Highly charged and emotionally laden issues for which people have strongly held positions are less likely to be subject to persuasion and more likely to be subject to polarization.

When Will Persuasion Occur?

Although Marshall (1989) and Rosenberg (1991) found little evidence of persuasive effects, this may be the result of their reliance on aggregate level data. As discussed more thoroughly in Chapter 1, aggregate data are not usually suitable for understanding how Court decisions affect individual level attitudes. Instead, the data for this chapter come from the two-wave panel studies conducted before and after four Supreme Court decisions in the local communities where the controversies began. As the discussion above and in the first chapter explains, research using aggregate data often does not provide a great deal of evidence that public opinion changes in response to Court decisions. Change often appears, but it is often inconclusive, in the opposite direction, or very muted. Certainly, no uniform pattern emerges when surveying the previous research. But, aggregate data are very good at masking individual level shifts.

Even Franklin and Kosaki (1989) and Johnson and Martin (1998) were not able to conduct true individual-level analyses. Instead, they relied on disaggregating cross-sectional data into groups. Also note how difficult it is to test the effect of confidence in the Court with these kind of data. Even though support for the Court is a theoretically important variable, its effect on support for Court decisions is difficult to analyze with these data (Grosskopf and Mondak 1998). It is one thing to identify Catholics (a relatively stable characteristic) in two sets of cross-sectional data. It is quite another to identify supporters of the Court at one wave and have confidence that they are the same group of people in a subsequent cross section. Membership in such a group may change over time, and importantly, may actually change in response to the Court decision of interest. Thus, it is virtually impossible to examine how support for the Court affects support for its decisions. Polarization, the pattern following abortion and capital punishment cases, is more likely to occur on issues where people already have strongly held beliefs on highly charged and controversial issues. Many of the Court's decisions, including the ones included in this research project, are not as contentious or politically charged as are abortion and the death penalty. Instead, many of these issues have important policy implications, but simply may not be the kinds of issues to which most Americans have given a great deal of thought. In short, while there is not a great deal of consensus, the experimental research holds the door open to the possibility that Court decisions can sway public opinion in the direction of its decisions, especially when we examine individual level changes and with the more typical kind of Court case – the kind included in this book.

So, while the Court may have the power of persuasion, is it reasonable to expect uniform patterns of persuasion across all individuals? The literature on persuasion suggests that we should not. Persuasion is affected by both individual and source characteristics. First and foremost, individuals must have exposure to the information. Chapter 3 showed that exposure to information was relatively high – extremely high in some cases – and that many people did learn about the Court's decisions as a result of having abundant information readily available.

But exposure is only the first thing to consider. What people do with the information once they receive it is equally important. Those who are able and motivated to spend time thinking about an issue are actually *less* likely to be persuaded than those who hear about it but spend less time thinking about the issue. Thinking through the issue, or having extensive prior information, enables individuals to generate counterarguments. Those who are less able and less motivated, but who still manage to hear about the information, are more likely to be persuaded. As important in the persuasion process is how the individual feels about the source of the message. Simply put, those with greater confidence in the source of the message (here, the Court) are more likely to be persuaded than those with less confidence in the institution. Each of these considerations helps generate the specific hypotheses detailed below.

THE DATA: LOOKING FOR CHANGES IN THE LOCAL COMMUNITIES

Simple Persuasion

Before testing the specific hypotheses about attitude change, it is important to first examine local public opinion on the issues in these cases before and after the Supreme Court handed down its decisions. Support for the issues is measured along a seven-point scale ranging from "very strongly disagree" with how the Court ultimately decided (1) to "very strongly agree" with how the Court ultimately decided (7). The exact questions

TABLE 4-1. *Support for the Supreme Court's Decision in the Four Panel Studies*

	Center Moriches	Monroe	Oklahoma	Oregon
First Wave	5.12	4.69	3.50	3.15
Second Wave	5.42	5.33	3.46	3.15
$p=$	.06	.001	.89	1.00
N	93	88	24	59

Note: Cell entries are mean level of support for the issue.

and response options are included in Appendix B. Higher values indicate greater support. In the Center Moriches case, higher values indicate support for the church's access to the school facilities. In the Monroe case, higher values indicate disagreement with the creation of a special school district for the Hasidic community. In Oklahoma, higher values indicate opposition to the state's collection of a fuel tax on gasoline sold by Native Americans. Finally, in the Oregon case, higher values indicate support for a broad interpretation of the Endangered Species Act that protects the habitat of the spotted owl and other endangered species.

If the Court exerts a simple persuasive effect on attitudes toward these issues, there would be greater support for the position the Court ultimately adopts. It is possible to examine such a simple persuasion effect by looking at support before and after the Court's decisions without taking into consideration any other factors, such as support for the Court or motivation to think about the issue. As Table 4-1 shows, there is mixed evidence to support a simple persuasion effect. In the Center Moriches sample, there is greater support for allowing church access to the school facilities following the decision than there was before the decision. In Monroe, too, there is greater support for eliminating the specially created school district after the decision than there was prior to the Court's decision. In Oklahoma and Oregon, however, there is no evidence of any opinion change at the aggregate level. So far, these results do not significantly depart from the aggregate research which shows little to no shifts in public support following a Court decision (e.g., Marshall 1989). Thus, either persuasion does not occur, or this test of persuasion simply does not capture all of the complexities of the persuasion process.

For a more complete picture of the distribution of changes in public opinion, there are graphs that measure the difference in seven-point scales between the first and second waves. Higher values indicate increased support for the position the Court takes. These graphs, presented in Figure 4-1, show that most people simply did not change their views. Typically in each of the four studies there was zero change in response from the first to the second interview. However, in Center Moriches and Monroe, it is clear that more people did change than in the other two studies, and that the change was more often positive than negative. This graph is consistent with the aggregate data presented above. In Oklahoma and Oregon, there are equal numbers of people who became more supportive as there are those who became less supportive. Even though these data offer some evidence for such a simple effect, it is far from convincing and tells us little about individual level responses to the Court's decisions.

Persuasion and Geographic Proximity

While there is some evidence to support a simple persuasion hypothesis, such an effect may be only part of the picture. After all, in each study – even Center Moriches and Monroe – some of the respondents actually became even *less* supportive. How might we account for these patterns? One factor to consider is whether the response of those from the immediate communities is different from those from the surrounding communities. Specifically, although it was somewhat mixed, the results from the previous chapter revealed that those from the immediate communities attached greater policy relevance to the issue than those from the surrounding communities. This finding was most consistent when respondents were asked how important they felt the issue was to their community. Thus, while the results were not quite as strong or uniform as hypothesized, those from the surrounding communities should still show more persuasion and those from the immediate community should show little to no persuasion effects. The first opinion change predicts the following hypothesis:

Opinion Change/Town of Residence Hypothesis: All else equal, those from the surrounding communities will change their opinion in the direction of the Court's decision more than those from the immediate community.

While Table 4-1 showed simple aggregate support for the Court's decision for the four surveys, Table 4-2 breaks down those results by whether the respondents are from the immediate or surrounding communities. Overall, there is only slight support for this hypothesis. In the Center Moriches study change was greater among those from the surrounding communities. Initially, the average score on this seven-point scale was 4.81, indicating just slight approval for allowing the church access to the high school's auditorium (four is the midpoint). After the decision, support for the church increased to 5.42. Upon learning about the Court's decision,

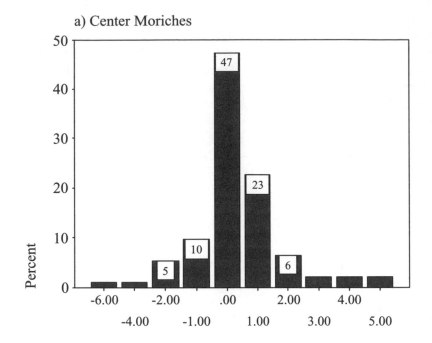

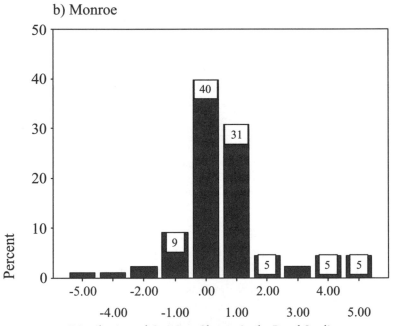

FIGURE 4-1. Distribution of Opinion Change in the Panel Studies.

c) Oklahoma

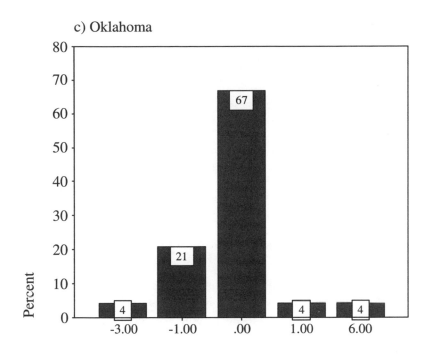

d) Oregon

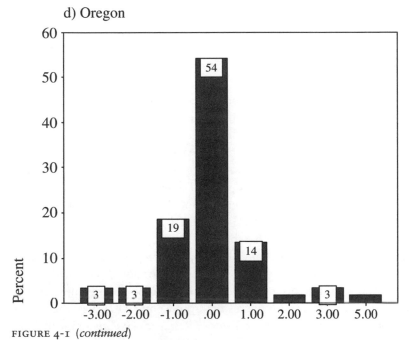

FIGURE 4-1 (*continued*)

TABLE 4-2. *Support for the Supreme Court's Decision in the Panel Studies by Geographic Proximity*

	Center Moriches	Monroe	Oklahoma	Oregon
Immediate Community				
First Wave	5.32	4.60	3.31	2.00
Second Wave	5.42	4.93	3.50	2.03
p=	.50	.16	.65	.87
N	57	40	16	35
Surrounding Communities				
First Wave	4.81	4.77	3.88	4.83
Second Wave	5.42	5.67	3.38	4.79
p=	.07	.00	.23	.90
N	36	48	8	24

Note: Cell entries are mean level of support for the issue.

overall opinion did shift in favor of allowing the church access to the auditorium. Remember that these are the individuals from the surrounding communities who are expected to hear about the decision, but to attach less significance to it than their counterparts in the immediate community. However, the difference is only marginally statistically significant ($p = .07$).

What about the residents from the immediate community? As expected, they showed a negligible change of only .10 on the seven-point scale, and this substantively small change was also insignificant statistically. Consistent with the *Opinion Change/Town of Residence Hypothesis*, this suggests that the overall change presented in Table 4-1 is largely driven by those who reside in the surrounding communities. So, while there are important differences between the immediate and surrounding communities, the simple aggregate results reported earlier masked those differences.

The results from the Monroe study are very similar. Again, Table 4-2 indicates that the residents of the surrounding communities became less supportive of the specially created school district (consistent with the Court's decision) than they were initially, by about one point on the seven-point scale. On the other hand, those from the immediate community of Monroe did not change their opinion regarding the creation of the school district. Residents who were initially opposed remained just as strongly opposed, and those who were initially supportive remained just as strongly supportive. As with the results from Center Moriches, the results here support the *Opinion Change/Town of Residence Hypothesis* nicely. But, support for the *Opinion Change/Town of Residence Hypothesis* ends with these two studies. In the Oregon and Oklahoma studies, breaking the data down by geographic proximity does not affect the results.[2] The outcome of those two studies points to the need to look beyond aggregate patterns.

Persuasion and Source Credibility

Thus far, there is only mixed evidence for either a more simple pattern of persuasion or a more complex pattern that takes into consideration geographic proximity to the case. However, the analysis has yet to consider another theoretically important variable: support for the Court. The persuasion literature shows that those who hold the Court in higher esteem should be much more likely to be persuaded by a Court decision (Petty and Cacioppo 1986; Fiske and Taylor 1992; see also Mondak 1990, 1992, 1994; Hoekstra 1995). In other words, support for the Court acts as an additional piece of evidence when individuals think about an issue. A message from a reputable and esteemed source has greater credibility than the same message from a less reputable and less well esteemed source. This leads to the following hypothesis:

Opinion Change/Support for Court Hypothesis: Those with initially higher levels of support for the Court should show greater change in the direction of the Court's decision than those with lower levels of support for the Court.

The initial test of this hypothesis simply takes the difference between how the individual initially felt about the issue and how that person felt about the issue following the Court's decision. This is the same opinion change score examined previously and in Table 4-2. Again, positive values of this variable, *Opinion Change*, indicate that the individual became increasingly supportive of the position the Court ultimately adopted. The other variable, *Support for the Court*, is also measured along a seven-point scale, where the value 1 indicates the lowest level of support ("very strongly disapprove") and 7 indicates the highest level ("very strongly approve"). This measure was created from two questions that were posed during both interviews. First, respondents were asked, "*In general, do you approve or disapprove of the way the Supreme Court is handling its job?*"

---

[2] This result is consistent with earlier research (Hoekstra 1995). In that experimental study, the Court was more persuasive when deciding a civil liberty case than an economic case. This may be due to the Court having greater legitimacy in civil liberties than economics. If so, then its credibility, an important source characteristic, lends it greater persuasive ability in one issue area than another. That speculation is consistent with the findings here. However, it is difficult to make too much of that observation without stronger theoretical or empirical support.

TABLE 4-3. *Relationship between Support for the Supreme Court and the Direction of Opinion Change*

	Center Moriches	Monroe	Oklahoma	Oregon
Correlation	.07	.07	−.10	−.03
$p=$	.25	.25	.32	.42
N	93	88	24	59

Note: Cell entries are correlation coefficients for the relationship between change in opinion on the issue and first-wave support for the Court. Probability based on one-tailed hypothesis tests.

Next, they were asked, "*Do you approve/disapprove very strongly, strongly, or not strongly?*" The seven-point scale was created from the combined responses.

What should result, according to the *Opinion Change/Support for Court Hypothesis*, is a positive relationship between these two variables: Those who like the Court should show greater change in support for the issue. Table 4-3 presents the results. In stark contrast with the hypothesis, there is absolutely no relationship between *support for the Court* and the structure of individual level *opinion change*. Those who hold the Court in high regard were no more likely to show greater support for the Court's decision than those who have very little regard for the Court. Even using relatively relaxed tests (these are one-tailed hypothesis tests), the relationship is not statistically significant. Moreover, the relationship is actually in the opposite direction in the Oklahoma and Oregon studies (−.10 and −.03 respectively).

However, since the *Opinion Change/Town of Residence Hypothesis* predicts that those from the surrounding communities should be more susceptible to persuasion, the next step is to examine the relationship between *opinion change* and *support for the Court* for the different geographic communities. These results are shown in Table 4-4. As this table shows, nothing changes by breaking the sample down by geographic community. Again, as with looking at the communities as a whole, there appears to be little or no evidence that *support for the Court* is related to *opinion change*. The relationship actually appears to be a negative one among the residents of the immediate community in the Oregon spotted owl case, and among the residents of both the immediate and the surrounding communities in the Oklahoma gasoline tax case.

These results are surprising and unexpected. While previous analyses showed positive change in only two of the four studies, some change did exist in all four. Yet, the change in those studies, whether toward greater

TABLE 4-4. *Relationship between Support for the Supreme Court and the Direction of Opinion Change by Geographic Community*

	Center Moriches	Monroe	Oklahoma	Oregon
Immediate Community				
Correlation	.00	.03	−.04	−.10
p=	.50	.43	.45	.28
N	57	40	16	35
Surrounding Communities				
Correlation	.13	.10	−.14	.06
p=	.23	.24	.37	.39
N	36	48	8	24

Note: Cell entries are correlation coefficients for the relationship between change in opinion on the issue and first-wave support for the Court. Probability based on one-tailed hypothesis tests.

or less acceptance of the Court's decision, does not appear to be related to *support for the Court*. This means that someone who approved of the Court was just as likely to become more supportive of the position the Court took as that individual was to become less supportive. The same is true for those who disapproved of the Court. This is so even among those from the surrounding communities who were expected to be most susceptible to persuasion by the Court. How can this finding be explained?

One potential explanation is that even in those two studies where there was some evidence of persuasion, there was not a great deal of variation in *opinion change*. After all, in Center Moriches 47 percent of the respondents did not adjust their opinion in either direction and nearly as many in Monroe, a full 40 percent, held onto their initial opinion. Moreover, those who did move on the scale are all clustered around a difference of only one point on the seven-point scale. Thus, there is little change to explain in the first place.

Another possible reason why no relationship emerges in the data might be due to lack of variation in *support for the Court*. This explanation is especially important to consider since most accounts show that the public tends to express high and enduring levels of confidence in the institution. There may be some merit to this argument. Chapter 5 discusses support for the Court in more detail, but for now, support among the residents of these four communities is detailed by the data graphed in Figure 4-2.

The graph shows that in two of the studies, Monroe and Oklahoma, there is not a great deal of variation in *support for the Court*. The most common response is strong approval of the Court (a score of six on a

a) Center Moriches

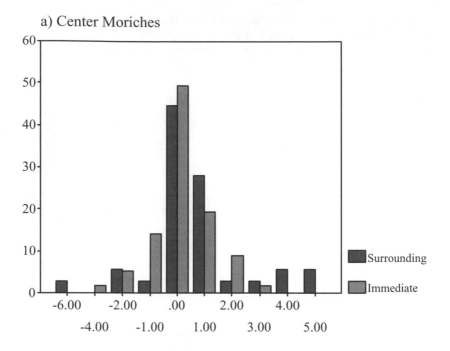

b) Monroe

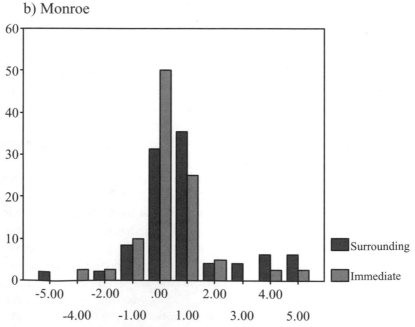

FIGURE 4-2. Distribution of Opinion Change in the Panel Studies by Geographic Proximity.

c) Oklahoma

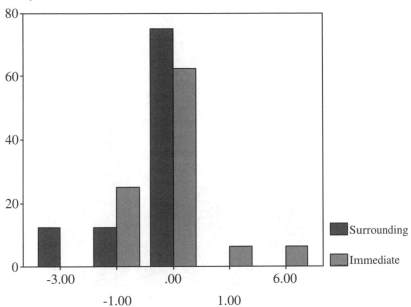

d) Oregon

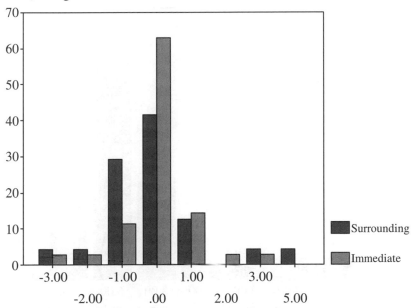

FIGURE 4-2 (*continued*)

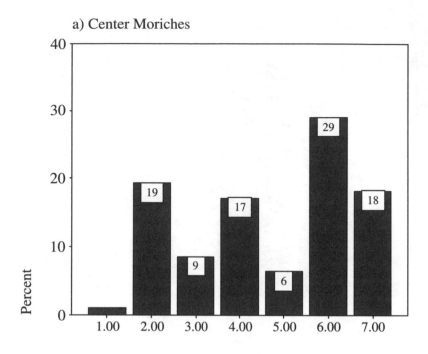

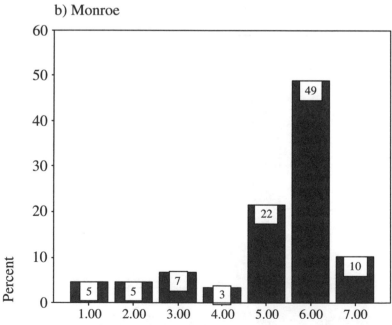

FIGURE 4-3. Distribution of Support for the Court in the Panel Studies (First Wave).

c) Oklahoma

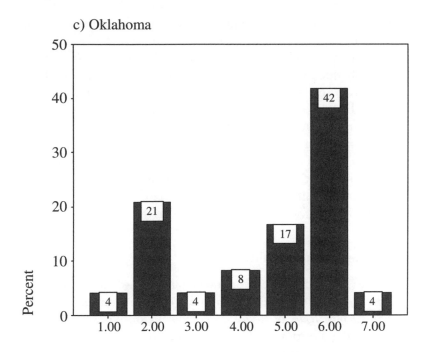

d) Oregon

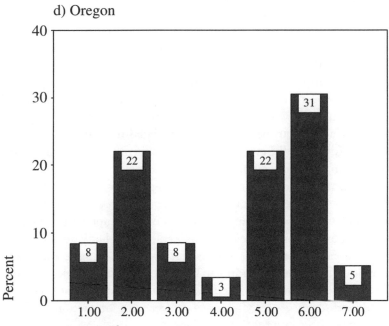

FIGURE 4-3 (*continued*)

seven-point scale). There is only slightly more variation in the other two studies – Center Moriches and Oregon. Thus, the lack of a relationship between these two variables – *opinion change* and *support for the Court* – may be partially due to the lack of variation in these two key variables. But, the variation (or lack thereof) does not completely correlate with the lack of findings. Recall that the lack of evidence for persuasion was most notable in the Oklahoma and Oregon studies, but that the lack of *variation in support* for the Court was most prominent in the Center Moriches study. However, in all four studies there was very little variation in *opinion change*. Another plausible explanation is that the process may still not be captured fully and that more systematic controls need to be introduced to account for the effects of other variables.

Multivariate Analysis and Results

Thus far there is some evidence of opinion change, mostly in the two civil liberty cases: Center Moriches and Monroe. There was some support for the *Opinion Change/Town of Residence Hypothesis* since positive change (i.e., change in the direction of the Court's decision) was more common among the residents of the surrounding communities in these two studies than it was among the residents of the immediate communities. The residents of the surrounding communities attached less policy relevance to the decision, and therefore did not evaluate the information in the Court's decision as critically as those from the immediate community.

Contrary to expectations – specifically the *Opinion Change/Support for the Court Hypothesis* – there was no evidence that support for the Court helps explain much of what was going on in the studies. In fact, support for the Court appears to be completely unrelated to change in support for the issue. Although the evidence is not very encouraging, the bivariate relationships may be misleading.

For the remainder of this chapter, the dependent variable in all of the multivariate analyses is the *Opinion Change* measure used previously. Again, this variable is simply the difference between support for the policy at the first and second waves of measurement. Higher values indicate an increase in support for the position that the Court adopts, and lower values indicate a decrease in support. The independent variables include: *Support for the Court, Town of Residence, Initial Opinion on the Issue*, and finally, *Support for the Court*Town of Residence* (an interaction between support for the court and town of residence).

The expectations of *support for the Court* are straightforward. Those who approve of the Court are expected to become, on average, more supportive of the Court's position. *Support for the Court* is measured on the seven-point scale described previously, but here the variable is recoded so that −3 indicates "very strong disapproval" and +3 indicates "very strong approval." The coefficient should be positive.

The analysis also includes the respondents' *town of residence* – (o) if they reside in the immediate community and (1) if they reside in the surrounding communities. A relatively simple persuasion hypothesis suggests that since those in the surrounding communities attached less significance to the issue, on average, they should become more supportive of the issue than those from the immediate communities. If there is support for the hypothesis, the coefficient should be positive. But, it is also included to test for an interactive effect with *support for the Court.* Specifically, this tests the final hypothesis initially introduced in Chapter 1.

Town of Residence/Court Support Interaction Hypothesis: The effect of support for the Court on opinion change should be conditioned on respondents' town of residence.

This final hypothesis predicts that while respondents' attitudes on the issue will be affected by how they feel about the Court, the effect should be greatest for those who reside in the surrounding communities. Therefore, the effect of *support for the Court* should be greatest among these individuals and the coefficient should be positive. Finally, the analysis includes respondents' *initial opinion on the issue* in order to control for any regression to the mean, which is the tendency for extreme values to become less extreme on subsequent measurements (Markus 1990; Finkel 1995).[3] Thus, the resulting coefficient should be negative.

The results from the multivariate analysis, shown in Table 4-5, do not paint a much more encouraging picture of the Court's persuasive appeal than did the bivariate results. The only variable included in the analysis to have any systematic effect across the four studies is the respondents' *initial opinion on the issue.* About 62 percent (Center Moriches) to 77 percent

---

[3] Since initial values may be negatively related to subsequent values, the coefficient should be negative. The coefficient has a substantive interpretation as well. A simple transformation of the coefficient $(1+\beta)$ provides information about the stability of respondents' attitudes toward the issue. The number that results from this transformation is exactly the same as current level of support was regressed on prior level of support for the issue (i.e., as if the dependent variable was the simple seven-point scale rather than the differenced dependent variable) (see Finkel 1995). For example, if in the change specification (with change as the dependent variable) the coefficient on initial opinion was estimated to be −.25, this tells us that some portion of the change is due to stability in the respondents' opinion on the issue $(1 + [−.25] = .75)$. This would tell us that about 75 percent of current attitudes on the issue is explained by respondents' prior opinions.

TABLE 4-5. *Multivariate Analysis of Opinion Change on the Issues in the Cases*

	Center Moriches	Monroe	Oklahoma	Oregon
Initial Opinion on the Issue	$-.38^{***}$	$-.35^{***}$	$-.23^{*}$	$-.25^{***}$
	(.09)	(.07)	(.13)	(.07)
Support for the Court	$-.01$	.16	.00	.01
	(.11)	(.16)	(.20)	(.10)
Town of Residence	.34	$.70^{*}$	$-.27$	.58
	(.32)	(.41)	(.79)	(.38)
Support for the Court*	$-.04$	$-.06$	$-.25$	.09
Town of Residence	(.16)	(.21)	(.44)	(.18)
Constant	$.62^{**}$	.34	.03	$-.48$
	(.23)	(.30)	(.38)	(.25)
F	6.05	6.69	1.15	3.16
Probability of F	.00	.00	.36	.02
Adjusted R^2	.18	.21	.03	.13
N	93	88	24	59

Note: $^{***}p < .001$. $^{**}p < .01$, $^{*}p < .05$, one-tailed hypothesis test.

(Oklahoma) of the change in respondents' support for the issue is explained by their *initial opinion on the issue*. None of the other variables, except *town of residence* in the Monroe study, help explain any of the remaining variation in changes in support for these issues. Holding all of the other variables constant, those from the surrounding communities in the Monroe study changed their opinion in the direction of the Court's ruling (against the operation of the school district) by nearly one full point (.70). This is consistent with the bivariate findings presented earlier. However, this effect only appears in one study. None of the other variables, including *support for the Court*, or the interaction between *town of residence and support for the Court*, explain the patterns of change on the issues.

EXPLORING THE LACK OF PERSUASION – THE ROLE OF EXPOSURE
TO INFORMATION AND EDUCATION

Exposure to Information

The disappointing and surprising lack of findings suggests that even this multivariate specification might be too simplistic. Persuasion, or other patterns of change, may be a function of other variables such as how often the respondents encountered the information and how well they were able to process and critically evaluate the information. Although everyone included in this analysis heard about the decision at least once, the extent of media coverage of the stories in these communities suggests that some people may have been exposed to information about the decision on more than one occasion. There was also substantial variation in media coverage between the communities, producing different levels of awareness.

Recall from the previous chapter that knowledge levels were much higher in Center Moriches and Monroe than in the Oregon and Oklahoma studies. Differences in exposure could very well produce different kinds of responses. High levels of exposure to information could result in greater persuasion if the individual hears the message often, but not so often as to be able to generate a sufficient store of counterarguments. Those who hear the message many times might, at some point, become better able to generate counterarguments (Petty and Cacioppo 1986; Fiske and Taylor 1992). Since it is virtually impossible to know just where that saturation point lies, there are no strong a priori expectations about the direction of this effect. However, it seems unlikely that the extent of media coverage, on its own, would be enough to make people resistant to persuasion. In some of these cases, particularly the Monroe and Center Moriches cases, there was indeed extensive media coverage of the decision. And yet, the majority of the coverage took place in a very brief span of time – just a few days. Thus, attention to politics should most likely increase the probability of persuasion.

In order to examine how exposure to information affects responses to Supreme Court decisions, an additional model that includes a measure of attention to politics was estimated. This variable, *attention to politics*, is a summary measure of three individual questions included in the survey instrument. Each of these questions asks respondents, *"How many days in the last week did you:* 1) *read a daily newspaper?,* 2) *watch the news on television?,* and 3) *discuss politics with friends or family members?"* Each of these variables ranges from 0 days to 7 days. Thus, *attention to politics* ranges from a possible low of 0 to a possible high of 21. The exception is the Center Moriches study. In that study, only two measures of attention were included on the instrument: reading the newspaper and watching the news on television. Therefore, in the Center Moriches study, the variable ranges from 0 to 14. All of the other variables included in the previous analysis are carried over. Table 4-6 shows the results for the analysis that includes attention to politics.[4]

---

[4] The argument about attention to politics is similar to the argument Segal and I (1996) present in our research on the Court's persuasive ability in our earlier analysis of the Center Moriches study. In that article, we were interested in examining the conditions

TABLE 4-6. *Multivariate Analysis of Opinion Change on the Issues in the Cases Controlling for Attention to Politics*

	Center Moriches	Monroe	Oklahoma	Oregon
Initial Opinion on the Issue	−.38**	−.41***	−.25*	−.28***
	(.09)	(.08)	(.14)	(.07)
Support for the Court	−.01	.16	.00	.02
	(.11)	(.32)	(.20)	(.10)
Town of Residence	.34	.70*	−.15	.67*
	(.32)	(.40)	(.92)	(.38)
Support for the Court*	−.04	−.07	−.28	.07
Town of Residence	(.17)	(.21)	(.46)	(.17)
Attention to Politics[a]	.00	.07**	−.03	d.06*
	(.03)	(.03)	(.09)	(.03)
Constant	.60	−.44	.33	−1.16**
	(.42)	(.48)	(1.12)	(.46)
F	4.78	6.84	.89	3.23
Probability of F	.00	.00	.51	.01
Adjusted R^2	.17	.26	−.02	.16
N	93	88	24	59

Note: *** $p < .001$. ** $p < .01$, * $p < .05$, one-tailed hypothesis test.
[a] In the Center Moriches study, the attention variable includes only the newspaper and television news measures and therefore ranges from 0 to 14.

Including a measure of the respondents' *attention to politics* does not dramatically change the picture. Again, among the main variables of interest (*support for the Court, town of residence,* and the interaction between these two) the results are weak. The finding of greater support for the Court's decision among the residents of the surrounding communities in the Monroe study remains positive, even with the measure of *attention to politics* included in the analysis. In addition, the effect now appears positive and significant in the Oregon study as well. Thus, there is slightly more evidence for the *Town of Residence/Court Support Interaction Hypothesis*. However, none of the other variables included in the previous analysis – except *initial opinion on the issue* – help explain opinion change.

under which the Court could persuade citizens and therefore we only looked at those who became more supportive compared to those who did not (i.e., either they did not change or they became less supportive). That decision was based on the findings that persuasion was the predominant structure of change following the decision. In that analysis we also include measures of the respondents' level of education and the strength of opinion. Those variables did not have any consistent effect on change (rather than persuasion) in opinion in all four of the studies. They also do not change the basic findings presented in Table 4-5.

At the same time, something important emerges from this analysis – the effect of *attention to politics*. Although it is significant in only two of the studies – Monroe and Oregon – the frequency with which respondents tuned into the news and discussed politics increased their exposure to information about the Court's decision, and, this increased their support for the Court's decision. To get a better understanding of just how *attention to politics* affects responses to Court decisions, consider two hypothetical people, John and Joe. Both John and Joe are from the Oregon sample and are similar in every respect except their tendency to pay attention to politics. John watches the news every evening (7), reads the paper just about every other day (3), and discusses politics on the weekends (2). Joe, on the other hand, only reads the paper on Sunday morning (1), never watches the news (0), and steers clear of political discussions (0). John's exposure to politics will cause him to become nearly one full point more supportive of the Court's decision ($[7 + 3 + 2] * .06 = .72$), but apparently Joe has not heard enough for him to change his mind on the issue ($1*.06=.06$). A similar but slightly larger effect is found in the Monroe study. However, accounting for individual level *attention to politics* had no discernible effects in either the Center Moriches or Oklahoma studies. Thus, while *attention to politics* was uniformly important in predicting and explaining who *heard* about the decision (see Chapter 4), it had only mixed effects on whether those people who heard about the decision were persuaded by it. It was important in two instances – Monroe and Oregon – but not in the other two – Center Moriches and Oklahoma.

Education

The lack of consistent findings between the studies may be the result of the effect of education on attitude change. Chapter 2 noted the differences in educational achievement both within the samples (immediate versus surrounding communities) and also between the four longer samples. Also, most likely there is variation in education at the individual level within a given sample, suggesting that education might need to be included in the analysis. While *attention to politics* might increase the Court's persuasive ability, those who are better educated might be able to create counterarguments, reducing their susceptibility to a persuasive message. Since *attention to politics* might be related to education, and since education might have an important effect on its own, the final analysis includes a variable measuring the respondents' level of education.

TABLE 4-7. *Multivariate Analysis of Opinion Change on the Issues in the Cases Controlling for Attention to Politics and Education*

	Center Moriches	Monroe	Oklahoma	Oregon
Initial Opinion on the Issue	−.39**	−.41***	−.77*	−.29***
	(.09)	(.08)	(.34)	(.08)
Support for the Court	.00	.16	.13	.02
	(.11)	(.16)	(.19)	(.10)
Town of Residence	.30	.70	−.09	.68*
	(.32)	(.43)	(.83)	(.38)
Support for the Court*	.00	−.07	−.58	.07
Town of Residence	(.17)	(.22)	(.44)	(.17)
Attention to Politics[a]	.00	.07**	.06	.06*
	(.04)	(.03)	(.09)	(.03)
Education	−.18	.01	−.33**	.04
	(.14)	(.15)	(.14)	(.16)
Constant	1.22*	−.45	2.07	−1.23*
	(.63)	(.61)	(1.23)	(.69)
F	4.30	5.63	1.80	2.66
Probability of F	.00	.00	.16	.03
Adjusted R^2	.18	.25	.17	.15
N	93	88	24	59

Note: *** $p < .001$. ** $p < .01$, * $p < .05$, one-tailed hypothesis test.
[a] In the Center Moriches study, the attention variable includes only the newspaper and television news measures and therefore ranges from 0 to 14.

This new variable, *education*, is measured along a five-point scale, coded as follows: (1) less than a high school education, (2) high school diploma, (3) some college, (4) college degree, (5) some post-graduate education. Since *education* should increase one's ability to counterargue and decrease one's reliance on simple source cues, the coefficient should be negative. The effect of *attention to politics* should come through more clearly and consistently after controlling for *education*. The results from this analysis are presented in Table 4-7.

Education decreased individual susceptibility to persuasion in two studies – Center Moriches and Oklahoma – but was significant in only one – Oklahoma. All else equal, in Oklahoma, respondents with more education were less likely to change their opinion in the direction of the Court's ruling than those with less education. The results for *attention to politics* remained the same. In both the Oregon and Monroe studies, the more exposure to the media and political discussions, the greater the likelihood of opinion change in the direction of the Court's decision, even after controlling for *education*. Another important difference from the previous analyses emerged. The effect of *town of residence* among those in the Monroe study, which was previously found to be an important explanatory variable, nearly disappeared. Once controls for *education* were introduced, those from the surrounding communities in the Monroe study were no longer more likely to change their opinion in the direction of the Court's decision. The variable *town of residence* is now only marginally significant.

CONCLUSION AND DISCUSSION

This chapter began with the words of Justice Sandra Day O'Connor from her opinion in the case of *Planned Parenthood of Southeastern Pennsylvania v. Casey* (1992). She referred to the Court's legitimacy as the power to command acceptance of it decisions. Is she right? Can the Court expend its legitimacy in order to help mold and shape public reactions? The evidence presented in this chapter is mixed. The Court does have a great deal of support among members of the mass public; however, this cache of legitimacy does not translate well into greater public acceptance of its decisions.

In two of the studies – Center Moriches and Monroe – there was initial evidence of some overall movement toward the position the Court took in its decisions. In Center Moriches, more people showed support for allowing the church to use the school facility, and in Monroe there was less support for the creation of the specially created school district after the Court decisions. In the other two studies, however, there was no evidence of any overall shift in one direction. Yet, given the complex nature of attitude change, a simple persuasion process is probably not realistic. The structure of opinion change was expected to be explained better by how strongly the individuals felt about the issue and also how they felt about the Court. Those with favorable opinions about the Court should have become more supportive of the Court's position, and those with less favorable attitudes toward the Court should have become less supportive. In addition, this effect was expected to be contingent upon whether the respondent was from the immediate or surrounding communities. However, this was not the case. Instead, how individuals felt about the Court – regardless of where they lived – did not explain how they reacted, if at all, to the Court's decision.

Slightly more encouraging and according to expectation were the results for the effect of attention to politics. There was some evidence, particularly in the Monroe and Oregon studies, that those who pay more attention to politics and the media – and presumably encountered more and/or repeated information about the Court's decision – did, on average, become more likely to change their opinions on the issue in the direction of the Court's decision. This result is consistent with the persuasion literature, which suggests that exposure to information is critical to bringing about opinion change. This effect remained even after controlling for level of education; however, this result appeared in only two of the four studies. But it does point to an interesting question about whether the Court's reluctance to create more and easier access to its decisions is a useful or wise strategy. If more information leads to greater acceptance of its decisions, it seems counterproductive for the Court to remain so well hidden. Why then, do the justices cling to their remoteness? One explanation is that while more media exposure of the decision may help increase compliance with the Court's decisions, it may also risk the Court's legitimacy among those who initially disagreed and who remain unpersuaded by their decision – a question addressed in the next chapter.

In short, while there was often extensive media coverage followed by high levels of public attention to the Court's decisions, neither one increased public acceptance of the Court's decisions consistently across the four studies. If there is good news for the Court, it is that citizens did not become less supportive. If there was any shift, it was, on balance, toward greater change in support of its decisions. But that shift was small and does not indicate that the Court can easily create a favorable environment for its decisions when the initial opinion is unfavorable.

But it is important to keep in mind that prevailing public opinion was not necessarily unfavorable to begin with in the communities where these cases originated. As is often true in American politics, opinion on the issues in these four cases was divided. Some of the residents supported the Court's position while others were opposed. Quite possibly, as long as there is a critical mass of support for the policy at the outset, the Court may not need to worry too much about shaping public opinion in those communities. On the other hand, the Court may face another dilemma. Though it was only able to modestly shape public opinion on the issues in these four communities, it is possible that these decisions affected levels of support for the Court. This is the central question addressed in the following chapter.

5

Public Support for the Supreme Court

> Whatever may be the merits or demerits of a poll-driven executive or a poll-driven legislature, the specter of a poll-driven judiciary is not an appealing one. So the search for greater public trust and confidence in the judiciary must be pursued consistently with the idea of judicial independence.
>
> – Chief Justice William H. Rehnquist[1]

INTRODUCTION

Chief Justice Rehnquist raises an important issue. Many scholars believe that while the members of the Court need not rely on public support in the same way as legislators or other elected officials, the specter of public disapproval apparently still looms large. Why should the justices care about public support if they are appointed to life tenured positions, cannot be overturned by any higher court, and are not likely to pursue higher office? The most important reason they should care is that public trust and confidence are precious political resources. Recall Felix Frankfurter's words in *Baker v. Carr* from Chapter 1. In that case, he said, "The Court's authority – possessed of neither the purse nor the sword – ultimately rests on sustained public confidence in its moral sanction." Public confidence can harbor the institution from attacks initiated by other branches of government and may also increase the likelihood of compliance with its decisions. But, the question remains as to whether popular decisions increase confidence in the Court and whether unpopular decisions decrease public confidence.

The discussion and results in this chapter are drawn from Hoekstra (2000).

[1] Rehnquist (1999, 9).

If Court decisions do not affect support for the institution, the justices need not worry about public reaction to those decisions. However, if they do, Rehnquist's concerns illustrate the problem they face. Namely, how does the Court maintain institutional independence without sacrificing public support? Since the results from the previous chapter show that Court rulings can, at best, only minimally and occasionally increase public support for the position the Court adopts, the critical issue is whether Court decisions can affect support for the institution. If so, judicial independence may be a very precarious commodity. If support for the Court is a function of its decisions, then the Court might not be able to resist public pressures for any length of time and may be subject to the same majoritarian pressures as the other branches of government.

Recall from the previous chapters that there were high levels of knowledge, but only little evidence that knowledge affected attitudes toward the issues. While there was some positive change, it was slight, inconsistent, and difficult to explain. There was evidence that individuals who pay attention to the news and frequently engage in political discussions were more likely to be persuaded than those who were less attentive. However, this was true in only two of the four samples – Monroe and Oregon. In short, the local media's coverage of the Court's decisions had little effect on how the people who read or saw the news reports felt about the issues in any consistent way. Had the Court been able to sway public opinion, implementation of the decision would have been much easier.

THE PERSISTENCE OF THE MINIMAL EFFECTS HYPOTHESIS

The question posed in this chapter boils down to this: Do Court decisions affect how the public feels about the Court? As evidenced by the quotes scattered throughout this book, the Justices believe support may indeed be tied to reactions to their decisions. And yet, most scholarly accounts of support for the Court, while not wholly dismissive of the role that its decisions play, are often reluctant to believe that decisions matter much as an ingredient in public support (Caldeira 1986; Mondak and Smithey 1997; Grosskopf and Mondak 1998; Kritzer 2001).

One reason for the endurance of this minimal effects hypothesis is that aggregate support for the Court is consistently high when compared with other institutions. This is true despite the fact that the Court often hands down controversial decisions (Franklin and Kosaki 1995; Hibbing and Theiss-Morse 1995; Marshall 1988, 1989). On the other hand, Congress and the president make controversial decisions; yet, approval of those two branches is always lower – often much lower for Congress – than is approval of the Supreme Court. Also, support for these other two branches appears to change, both positively and negatively, in response to events more often than does support for the Court. These two observations combined leave a picture of enduring Supreme Court popularity. It appears Supreme Court support is both relatively high and relatively stable. In addition, conventional wisdom assumes people do not know very much about the Court, which precludes the possibility of its decisions having much of an impact.

Probably the most enduring reason why scholars continue to believe that support for the Court is independent of its decisions is the fundamental difference between the Court and the other two branches of government. Most notably in the early research, there is a persistent view that the Court is simply different from other institutions and whatever yardsticks that might be used to measure Congressional or presidential support simply cannot be used to measure Supreme Court support.

These arguments have proven to be very compelling and have become part of conventional wisdom. But how thoroughly have they been investigated? Chapter 3 showed that the decisions were extensively covered by the local media (and to some extent by the national media) and that many people, more than is typically thought, heard about them. The high levels of awareness can be attributed to two influences. First, the local media attention to the local cases was extensive. Second, given the local importance of these cases, the residents had greater interest than would someone living elsewhere. These results should not be too surprising considering that Franklin, Kosaki, and Kritzer found similarly high levels of awareness in national samples when they timed their surveys to coincide with the Court's calendar (Franklin, et al. 1993; Franklin and Kosaki 1995; Kritzer 2001). Media coverage provided sufficient information, and people were interested enough in the cases to pay attention. In Franklin and his colleagues' research, the motivation to pay attention was driven by the highly salient nature of the issues. In the local community samples drawn for this book, interest was driven by the fact that these cases contained issues of local concern.

What about the relatively high and stable levels of support? Why does the Court enjoy such popularity? Why does that popularity seem immune to even the most controversial decisions? Do certain values or enduring beliefs about the Court insulate it from reactions to the policy outcomes of Court decisions? The aggregate data showing high and enduring levels of support surely seem consistent with the Court being immune. But, high and stable popularity in the aggregate is also consistent with the other explanation – that the decisions do, in fact, matter. While *aggregate* support might remain high and stable, *individuals* could be updating how they feel about the Court. This would be the case when some people become more supportive and an equal number become less supportive of the Court in response to its decisions. As Mondak and Smithey (1997) note, "... aggregate-level studies and broad propositions mask the fact that the public does not necessarily respond en masse to Supreme Court decisions" (1997, 1120; see also Kritzer 2001). Instead, group membership (i.e., race, religion, etc.) conditions responses. Moreover, if the Court chooses to take public opinion into account when rendering its decisions, as some recent research suggests (Mishler and Sheehan 1993, 1996; Stimson, et al. 1995; Flemming and Wood 1997; but see Norpoth and Segal 1994), its popularity can remain high even if individual decisions are unpopular with some segments of the population. In other words, with aggregate data, it may be impossible to rule out either explanation completely. These questions require individual level data. Undoubtedly, evaluations of the Court are not created out of whole cloth with each new decision. Support for the Court, as with any other institution, is probably a mixture of ingredients. But, individual level data is a better tool to examine the various components of support for the Court.

What about the fundamental uniqueness argument? Although scholars continue to be skeptical about the role Court decisions play in public evaluations of the Court, most people simply do not think about the Court in the same way they think about Congress or the President. To some extent, this must be true. The Court is fundamentally different: it has less visibility since the justices do not campaign for office; and, it conducts its business differently from the other two branches. But recognizing these differences does not mean abandoning explanations of public support for other institutions to create an entirely separate theory of support for the Court. The simple fact is that all three institutions create policy, often on some of the most contentious issues of the day. All three branches must make choices – choices that will undoubtedly please some and anger others. Once a policy or decision is made public, it has the potential to affect support for that particular institution.

This chapter examines changes in support for the Court among those who heard about the Court's decisions. The individual level panel data will shed light on this question in ways that aggregate data simply cannot and have not been able to answer adequately. In particular, the data will enable further exploration into whether agreement with the Court's decisions affects change in support for the Court. However, as a starting point for the analysis, it is crucial to understand the main theories of support for the Court.

THE CONNECTION BETWEEN COURT DECISIONS AND SUPPORT FOR THE COURT

Research on the relationship between specific Supreme Court decisions and public support for the Court has been frustrated by the apparent public ignorance of all but the most controversial and visible cases (Caldeira 1991). The standard account portrays citizens as quite willing to offer an opinion about the institution, even though they apparently do so without much information. Many scholars conclude that support for the Court rests upon more enduring attitudes about the legitimacy of the Court and its role in the system of government, rather than on agreement or disagreement with specific decisions. The problem, however, is that this theory relies heavily on the assumption that the public is indeed unknowledgeable. Chapter 3 casts doubt on this assumption. When media coverage is high, public knowledge can also be very high.

Most previous accounts suggest that the majority of Court decisions go unnoticed; still, the possibility that Court decisions influence attitudes remains an open question, in large part due to the findings from experimental research. In such research, the connection between institutional support and Court decisions has been well established (Mondak 1991, 1992; Segal 1995). It is only outside of the laboratory that this connection remains rather elusive (Mondak and Smithey 1997; Grosskopf and Mondak 1998; Kritzer 2001). The reason is straightforward: If people do not hear about Court decisions, by definition those decisions can have no impact. But, as revealed in Chapter 3, levels of awareness in the local communities were quite high, especially in the Monroe and Center Moriches cases, and it was often higher among those from the immediate communities. This provides a unique opportunity to examine this question under more realistic, real-world conditions.

Institutional Legitimacy

As discussed previously, many scholars remain skeptical about the role Court decisions play in determining that institution's popularity. Most accounts refer to the Court's legitimacy as an institution of government.

Explanations for the source of this legitimacy are diverse, but each can be traced back to Dahl's (1957) seminal work on the Court. Dahl suggested that the Court, rarely out of line with majoritarian preferences, lends legitimacy to the policies of other branches of government (rather than strikes them down). While Dahl was interested in a slightly different research question – whether the Court acts in a countermajoritarian fashion – an implicit assumption in his work was that the Court has legitimacy to bestow upon these policies, or at the very least, has more legitimacy than the other institutions whose policies stand to benefit from the Court's approval. While some of Dahl's conclusions have been subject to debate (Casper 1976), few question Dahl's assumption about the legitimacy of the Court. Most scholars recognize that the Court is consistently evaluated more positively than either Congress or the Executive branches of government. Dahl's work spawned at least two lines of inquiry: 1) the countermajoritarian question and 2) the legitimacy question. Those who pursued the legitimacy question turned toward understanding the underlying sources of support for the Court.

Early Research on the Special Role of the Court

The emphasis in much of the early research was that the Court benefits from socialization that leads citizens to perceive it is a "wise" and "benevolent" institution and as the last bastion of Constitutional freedoms (Easton 1965, 1975; Easton and Dennis 1969; Adamany and Grossman 1973; Casey 1974; Jaros and Roper 1980). Although people may not know much about the Court's recent activities according to this view, they have an idealized textbook version of the Court. Fundamental to this early research was an idea of the uniqueness of the Supreme Court among political institutions. Accordingly, citizens do not view the Court the same way that they view the political branches of government. Instead, the Court is evaluated by completely different criteria. Recently, Lyons and Scheb (2000) argued that members of the mass public tend to perceive Court decisions as legally rather than politically determined. Thus, even some recent research persists in arguing that the Court is different. According to this line of inquiry, attitudes toward the Court are viewed as fixed – once formed, it never changes. Although most recent research has largely abandoned the idea that the public perceives the Court in "mythical" terms, the ideas of this early line of research have solidly anchored researchers into the mind-set of the uniqueness of the Court. Rather than focus on the similarities between the Court and the other branches of government, the focus remains on the differences between the Court and the "political" branches.

Institutional Legitimacy – Specific and Diffuse Support

Much of the recent research on the Court has examined different sources of support for the Court. Easton's (1965, 1975; Easton and Dennis 1969) work on institutional legitimacy introduced the idea that there may be two different kinds of institutional support – specific and diffuse. According to Easton and subsequently others, diffuse support for the Court (or any institution) comes from relatively enduring attitudes, while specific support refers to support for the Court's (or other institution's) actions (Easton, 1965, 1975; Caldeira 1991; Caldeira and Gibson 1992; Gibson and Caldeira 1992; Segal 1995; Gibson, Caldeira and Spence 2002; see also Jaros and Roper 1980; Murphy and Tanenhaus 1968, 1970).

Diffuse support for the Court refers to "generalized and firm attachments" or a "reservoir of favorable attitudes" (Caldeira 1991, 322). As such, at the theoretical level diffuse support is an enduring characteristic that should lack a connection with the ideological or policy outputs of the Court. In other words, liberals will still support the Court even when the Court hands down conservative decisions, as long as the Court does not appear to be doing so for ideological reasons. If individuals have deeply held positive attitudes toward the Court (diffuse support), unpopular and controversial decisions can be set aside if those people believe the members of the Court came to their decision on a Constitutional or legal basis, rather than on their own policy preferences or at the behest of certain interests. On the other hand, specific support refers to a "set of attitudes toward an object based upon the fulfillment of demands for particular policies or actions" (Caldeira 1991, 322). In other words, the idea behind specific support is not whether one perceives the institution to be legitimate, but whether one is pleased with a specific decision.

Much of the research on specific and diffuse support focuses on measurement issues. Although they are thought to be theoretically distinct by many scholars, it has been difficult to devise scales that separately estimate the underlying constructs. In particular, Caldeira and Gibson (1992) developed numerous items designed to isolate these constructs. Their measures of diffuse support include questions about whether the respondent would support attempts to limit the powers of the Court in response to controversial and unpopular decisions. Their question tapping into specific support asks whether the respondent believes the Court to be either "too liberal, too conservative, or about right in its decisions" (Caldeira and Gibson 1992, 642).

The goals of this project are different from the goals in research on diffuse and specific support; therefore, this chapter will measure support differently from the way Caldeira and Gibson measure it. There are two fundamental reasons for this difference. First, it is possible for someone to lose confidence in an institution when they disagree with a decision, even if they would not press for fundamental changes in the institutional and constitutional powers of that institution. This change in confidence is not trivial. Even though citizens may not be ready to abolish the Court or limit its powers, a lack of confidence might still threaten the Court's ability to act independently and to induce compliance from other branches of government. Caldeira and Gibson's measures of diffuse support simply may not capture this sort of damage to the institution.

Second, support is measured differently because any observed relationship between Caldeira and Gibson's measures of diffuse and specific support might be explained as a measurement problem. In other words, if an empirical relationship was found, someone might argue that the underlying constructs were not being properly isolated. Instead, specific support is measured as support for a specific decision and support for the institution is measured by asking respondents about their confidence in the institution – specifically, whether they approve or disapprove of the Court (see Appendix B for exact question wording). This measurement approach is similar to the method others have chosen. Mondak and Smithey (1997) argue that such a measure falls somewhere in between diffuse and specific support.

Despite the different measurement strategies and goals, the extant research does not entirely preclude the impact of Court decisions. Rather, unlike some of the earliest research on support for the Court, there is assumed to be some dynamic component to the process, where especially notable or activist decisions may factor into the equation. Indeed, Caldeira and Gibson suggest just this: "... to the extent that the Supreme Court openly embraces judicial activism, the citizenry may judge the institution in the same light as other political institutions: policy agreement and disagreement will significantly affect support for the institution" (1992, 652).

Mondak and Smithey (1997) present a similar argument. Their mainly theoretical model of dynamic support for the Court suggests that while individual attitudes toward the Court generally tend to be positive, they may change as a result of controversial and unpopular decisions. While Caldeira and Gibson (1992) focus on judicial activism (which is theoretically unrelated to ideology, since both liberal and conservative decisions can be characterized as activist), Mondak and Smithey (1997) focus on controversial and unpopular decisions. Regardless of their specific differences, both accounts leave room for decisions to enter into the equation.

Support for Supreme Court Procedures – The "Process" Argument

Finally, still others argue that the Court's procedures, such as the secrecy of deliberations, infrequent media attention, and perceptions of being removed from partisan political battles both within the Court and between the Court and other branches of government, lend the Court greater public support (Hibbing and Theiss-Morse 1995). In other words, *process* is key to understanding support for political institutions, including the Court. Congress is a much reviled institution not simply because of dissatisfaction with the policies that come out of the institution, but also because of dissatisfaction with the way those policies are fashioned. Plainly stated, citizens have lost confidence in that institution since much of the information they encounter about it, often from their own representative, is negative. Scandals, infighting, party politics, and perceptions of undue interest group influence seem to dominate congressional politics. Hibbing and Theiss-Morse (1995) suggest:

Congress embodies practically everything Americans dislike about politics. It is large and therefore ponderous; it operates in a presidential system and is therefore independent and powerful; it is open and therefore disputes are played out for all to see; it is based on compromise and therefore reminds people of the disturbing fact that most issues do not have right answers. Much of what the public dislikes about Congress is endemic to what a legislature is. Its perceived inefficiencies and inequities are there for all to see (1995, 60).

In other words, Congress can be a nasty place. The president may similarly suffer if he gets caught up in such inter-branch battles. Intra-branch conflicts are less of a problem for the presidency. Whatever battles occur within the executive branch are not usually played on the public stage. According to this process argument, institutions are evaluated by the way they conduct their business as much as they are by what they produce. Similar sentiments have been expressed by Chief Justice William Rehnquist, who suggested that reforms in court procedures might help maintain high levels of public confidence in courts. Although he was referring to courts in general, his comments are consistent with the logic of the process argument (Rehnquist 1999).

What is so interesting and appealing about the process argument is that it provides a single theoretical framework for understanding public evaluations of institutions more generally. Unlike the earliest research on the "mythical" quality of the Court, or even to some extent the diffuse/specific support research, the process argument presents a theory that can be applied to all three political institutions. In fact, this is one of the primary goals articulated by Hibbing and Theiss-Morse (1995). As they note, there is virtually no research on support for political institutions in general, and even the research on the three institutions separately is lacking. The process argument's generalizability is much more intuitive and attractive than much of the early work on support for the Court.

As the name suggests, the process argument focuses more on process than on policy. However, it does not entirely dismiss the role of policy in support for institutions. Instead, the reason to look at process, according to Hibbing and Theiss-Morse (1995), is that it has been largely ignored in the research on Congress. However, in the research on the Court, it is the role of policy that has not received the attention it deserves. For these reasons, the process argument has a great deal to offer in better understanding support for political institutions. Anecdotal accounts and extant data tend to support this argument as well. Aggregate longitudinal data on support for the three institutions almost always show Congress as the least favored branch, the Supreme Court as the most favored, and the executive branch as somewhere in between (Marshall 1989; Hibbing and Theiss-Morse 1995; Mondak and Smithey 1997).

THE DATA AND EMPIRICAL EVIDENCE

The Most Popular Institution or the Lesser of Three Evils? Evidence from the Aggregate Data

Nearly every year since 1972, the General Social Survey (GSS) has asked a random sample of American citizens how they feel about a variety of American institutions and figures.[2] Included in this battery are questions about the legislative, the executive, and the judicial branches of government. The question wording is constant across the time span creating an ideal series with which to compare support. Specifically, the item

---

[2] The confidence question was not asked in the following years: 1972, 1979, 1981, 1985, and 1992. The survey was conducted biennially beginning in 1994, so there was no survey conducted in 1995 and 1997. Estimates are interpolated for those missing years.

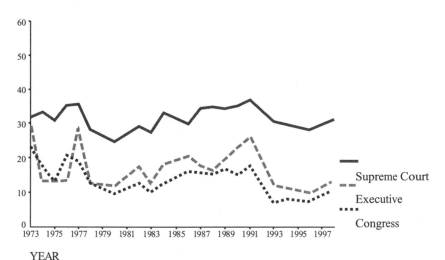

YEAR

FIGURE 5-1. Respondents Claiming "A Great Deal of Confidence in...." *Source:* Data from the General Social Survey. Confidence questions were not asked in 1972, 1979, 1981, 1985, and 1992. The survey was conducted biennially beginning in 1994, so there was no survey conducted in 1995 and 1997. Estimates are interpolated for those missing years.

states: "I am going to name some institutions in this country. As far as the people running these institutions are concerned, would you say you have a great deal of confidence, only some confidence, or hardly any confidence at all in them?" Respondents are then asked to rate Congress, the executive branch, and the Supreme Court, as well as numerous other people and institutions. Figures 5-1, 5-2, and 5-3 graph levels of support for each of the three institutions between 1973 and 1998.

Figure 5-1 shows that throughout this twenty-five-year period, the Supreme Court has always had more support than either Congress or the Executive branches. This is consistent with much of the previous research about aggregate support for the Supreme Court. Excluding the few years following the Watergate scandal, the Nixon presidency, and the resulting decline in public confidence in the executive branch, Congress almost always fares the worst. At that low water mark for executive approval, Congress managed to make a modest, though temporary gain in confidence, temporarily surpassing executive approval. Throughout nearly the entire series, more than 30 percent of the population claimed to have a "great deal of confidence" in the Supreme Court and it maintains a comfortable lead of approximately 10 to 15 percentage points over either of the other two – usually the president – at any point in time. Even during the so-called presidential honeymoon periods – roughly the first year a president is in office – and the corresponding spikes in executive approval, the Court maintained a healthy margin of citizens willing to claim that they have a "great deal of confidence" in the institution.

In the aggregate, it is clear that the Supreme Court can claim a healthy store of public confidence. So far, this is consistent with most accounts of the Court's legitimacy. But there is movement in all three of the series – movement that tracks together rather remarkably. From about 1977 to 1991, each series showed a gradual increase in public confidence. After 1991, they each moved in a similar, slightly downward trajectory. This is consistent with Caldeira's (1986) finding that suggests that the fates of all three institutions are tied to one another. Often, the public responds to events and circumstances and either gains or loses confidence in all three branches of government in tandem. While the absolute levels might be different, the changes appear to have something in common. So, while support for the Court is always higher than is support for the other two branches, confidence in it, as with the other two branches, does appear to respond to some external events. The spikes may not be as sharp in the Supreme Court series as they are in the other two, but they exist nonetheless.

Another important observation from Figure 5-1 is that if approximately 30 to 35 percent of the public has "a great deal of confidence" in the Supreme Court, somewhere between 65 and 70 percent express something less. This point is all but glossed over in most accounts of public support for the Court (but see Adamany and Grossman 1983; Caldeira 1986; Marshall 1989). Just how many people express "hardly any confidence" is shown in Figure 5-2. During this same twenty-five-year period, the number of people who claimed to have "hardly any confidence" in the Supreme Court hovered around 15 percent. It varies only slightly over time, suggesting that at any given moment, there are some who disapprove of the Court. Disapproval of the other two branches of government is consistently higher and more variable. While lack of confidence in the Supreme Court appears relatively stable, lack of confidence in Congress and the executive branch appears much more volatile as it shifts by approximately twenty-five percentage points.

When it comes to confidence in the three branches of government, the majority of Americans fall into the middle category, claiming to have "only some confidence." The number of Americans who fall into this category is graphed in Figure 5-3. Except for the mid-1990s, the most frequent response for all three branches is this middle category. In the

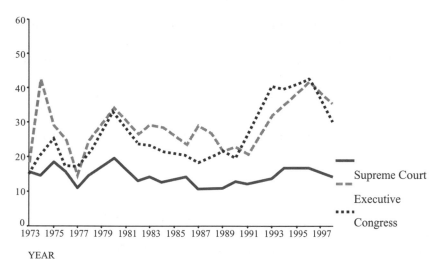

FIGURE 5-2. Respondents Claiming "Hardly Any Confidence in...." *Source:* Data from the General Social Survey. Confidence questions were not asked in 1972, 1979, 1981, 1985, and 1992. The survey was conducted biennially beginning in 1994, so there was no survey conducted in 1995 and 1997. Estimates are interpolated for those missing years.

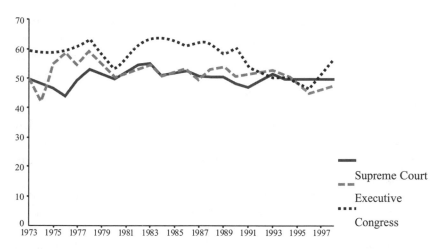

FIGURE 5-3. Respondents Claiming "Only Some Confidence in...." *Source:* Data from the General Social Survey. Confidence questions were not asked in 1972, 1979, 1981, 1985, and 1992. The survey was conducted biennially beginning in 1994, so there was no survey conducted in 1995 and 1997. Estimates are interpolated for those missing years.

1990s, there are nearly equal numbers of people with "only some confidence" in all three institutions. Clearly, the other two categories, "a great deal" and "hardly any," separate the three institutions in the aggregate. People probably move in and out of this middle-of-the-road category in response to actions by these institutions (Mondak and Smithey 1997).

Individual Level Change in Support for the Court – Results from the Panel Studies

The majority of research examining the bases of support for the Court relies on aggregate level data. As earlier discussions note, there has not been much evidence to suggest that changes in support for the Court are related to its decisions (but see Franklin and Kosaki 1995; Mondak and Smithey 1997; and Grosskopf and Mondak 1998). The main exception comes from experimental research, which finds evidence that there is a relationship between support for Court decisions and support for the Court (Mondak 1991, 1992; Segal 1995). In the laboratory setting, subjects update their evaluation of the Court based on how they feel about Court decisions. In other words, Court decisions matter.

However, as discussed more extensively in Chapter 1, scholars have had difficulty replicating these results beyond the experimental setting. First, there is the problem that if people do not know anything about Court decisions, the institution can have no effect. But Chapter 3 showed that many people can and do learn about Court decisions. Knowledge of two of the cases, Center Moriches and Monroe, was incredibly high. Overall, approximately 80 percent of the respondents in Center Moriches and 70 percent in Monroe knew about the Court's decision. In the other two cases, overall knowledge was somewhat lower, about 40 percent in the Oregon case and 20 percent in the Oklahoma case, but these figures are still higher than previous accounts report.

Second, and more importantly, generalizability from experimental studies may be limited by selection issues. While many people did learn about the Court's decisions in the panel studies, not everyone did. Those with higher levels of education were more likely to hear about the decisions. However, education also tends to lead people to have more stable or crystallized beliefs. Here is the problem: In the laboratory setting, *everyone* hears about Court decisions whether or not they are likely to do so in the real world. In the "real world," those with lower levels of education, and hence more malleable attitudes toward the Court (or any issue), are less likely to hear about a decision. What occurs in the lab may or may

TABLE 5-1. *Support for the Supreme Court in the Panel Studies*

	Center Moriches	Monroe	Oklahoma	Oregon
First Wave	4.69	5.20	4.54	4.20
Second Wave	–	5.01	4.80	4.08
N	93	88	24	59
p <	–	.19	.28	.62

Note: Entries are means. Statistical significance based on difference in means *t*-test.

not occur outside of the lab. The lesson from the experimental research is that Court decisions have the *potential* to affect perceptions of the Court. Individual level data need to be collected outside of the lab to see if this potential can be realized.

The first set of analyses using the individual-level data examines overall levels of support for the Court at the first and second waves. This is followed by an examination of attitudes toward the Court as a function of support for how the Court ultimately decided. Next is an examination of these relationships among those from the immediate and surrounding communities, as well as among those who did and did not hear about the Court's decisions, and also by respondents' level of education. In this analysis, *support for the Court* is measured along a seven-point scale, where (7) indicates "very strongly approve" and (1) represents those who "very strongly disapprove." Thus, higher values reflect stronger support for the Court. The aggregate measure of support for each of the four studies is presented in Table 5-1. Unfortunately, *support for the Court* was not included in the second wave of the Center Moriches study, so the table only shows how these respondents felt about the Court before the ruling.[3] As discussed above, there should not be any systematic changes from the first wave to the second wave just yet.

Overall, *support for the Court* is relatively high, as shown in Table 5-1. The average support for the Court in all four studies is always higher than the midpoint (4). The respondents from Monroe are the most supportive (5.20 and 5.01) and those in the Oregon samples are the least supportive – just above neutral (4.20 and 4.08). There are no statistically significant aggregate changes in support after the announcement

---

[3] The Center Moriches study served as a pilot study. The original research focus was the effect of Court decisions on public opinion (Chapter 4). After the initial pilot study, the focus of the research was broadened to include the question included in this chapter (i.e., the effect of Court decisions on support for the Court).

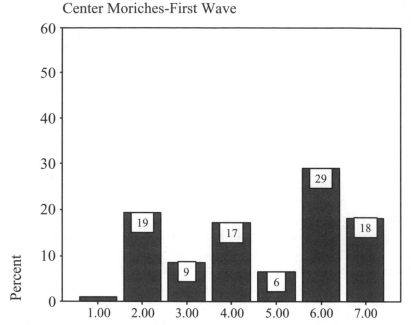

FIGURE 5-4. Distribution of Support for the Court in the Four Panel Studies.

of its decisions. In two of the studies (Monroe and Oregon) it decreases somewhat, and in Oklahoma there is a slight increase. Much like the aggregate GSS time series presented above, support within the panels is relatively high and stable.

A series of graphs helps to illustrate further how respondents felt about the Court. Those graphs, presented in Figure 5-4, reveal a pattern similar to the results in Table 5-1, as well as the results from the previous national data. For the most part, support for the Court is high. The most common response in all four studies is strong approval of the Court both before and after the Court's decision (a score of six on the seven-point scale). However, there are differences between the four studies and within them, between the first and second measurement. In Monroe, the most common response, by a wide margin, was strong approval of the Court both before (49 percent) and after (38 percent). A similar pattern unfolds in the Oklahoma panels. The most common response was strong approval of the Court both before (42 percent) and after (38 percent). Before the decision, however, there were quite a few (21 percent) who strongly disapproved. That number drops to 8 percent after the decision. The picture for those from Oregon is slightly different. Here, approval is

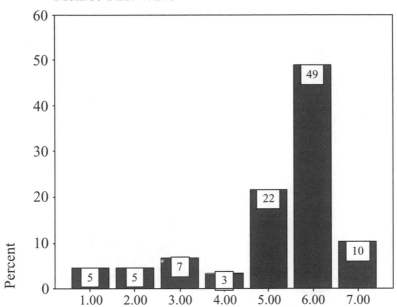

Monroe-First Wave

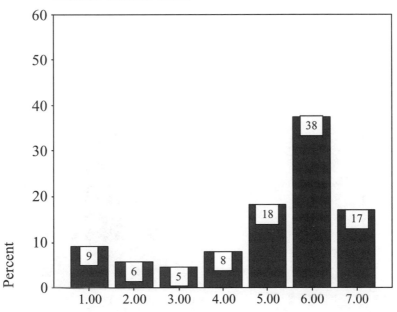

Monroe-Second Wave

FIGURE 5-4 (*continued*)

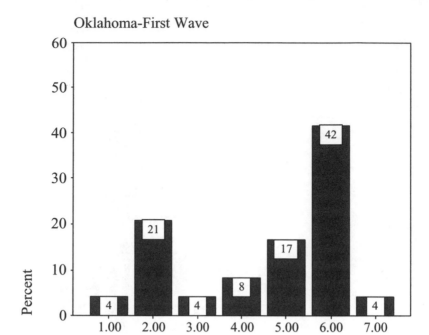

Oklahoma-First Wave

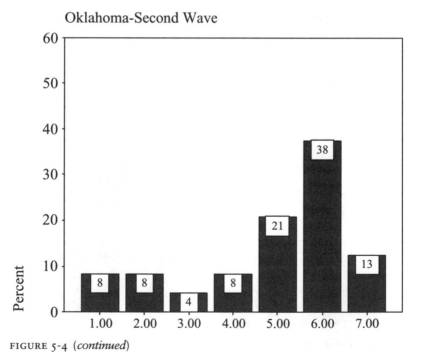

Oklahoma-Second Wave

FIGURE 5-4 (*continued*)

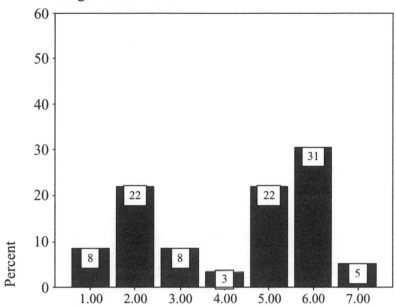

Oregon-First Wave

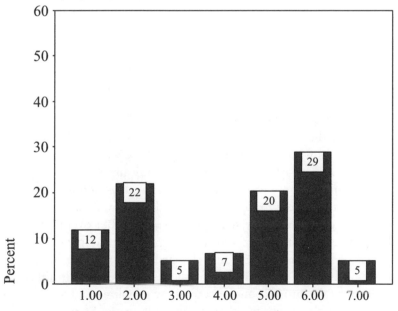

Oregon-Second Wave

FIGURE 5-4 *(continued)*

more widely dispersed. Strong approval is the most common response at both waves of measurement (31 and 29 percent respectively), but there is more variation in support in this study than in any of the other studies.

While there was no reason to expect to find any systematic changes in support for the Court at this point, some research suggests that activist and notable Court decisions might affect support even without considering support for the policy direction of the decision. Particularly, Caldeira and Gibson (1992) suggest that support for the Court as an institution (i.e., diffuse support) might suffer in the wake of controversial and activist decisions. Simply by placing itself in the midst of obviously political debates and by overturning the actions of democratically elected officials, the Court may risk its institutional legitimacy. Given the local salience of each of these cases – especially the Monroe case, which had such a contentious background and extensive local media coverage – and the Oregon case, pitting the environmentalists against the logging industry, some aggregate change was within the realm of possibility. Similarly, three of the four decisions – Center Moriches, Monroe, and Oklahoma – overturned legislation that was duly enacted by elected officials. Thus, if activism alone, without considering the direction of the policy, is an important ingredient in support for the Court, such patterns might emerge from the data. It is fairly clear that they did not. Instead, we need to consider the direction of the Court's decisions and whether the respondents agreed or disagreed with the policy that the Court ultimately adopted.

The first step in disaggregating the results is to examine *support for the Court* among and between the different geographic samples. Again, even though this analysis begins to disaggregate somewhat, there should not necessarily be any predictable changes as of yet because support for the policy outcome has not been taken into account. Table 5-2 shows change in support for those who reside in the immediate and the surrounding communities. As with the previous findings, there was not much significant change in *support for the Court*. The only instance of significant change was among those who reside in the immediate community in the Oklahoma sample – the residents of Ada, Oklahoma. And even in Ada, the change is only marginally significant ($p = .09$). But overall, the lack of change was not surprising and did not preclude the possibility that individual perceptions of the Court changed in response to its actions. While this is disaggregated further than the results presented in Table 5-1, it still did not take into account whether these people agreed or disagreed with the Court's decision. In other words, systematic differences at this level of disaggregation are not likely to emerge.

TABLE 5-2. *Support for the Supreme Court in the Panel Studies by Geographic Community*

	Center Moriches	Monroe	Oklahoma	Oregon
Immediate Community				
First Wave	4.67	5.20	4.25	3.83
Second Wave	–	4.93	4.69	3.86
N	57	40	16	35
$p=$	–	.27	.09	.94
Surrounding Community				
First Wave	4.72	5.21	5.13	4.75
Second Wave	–	5.08	5.25	4.42
N	36	48	8	24
$p=$	–	.47	.88	.26

Note: Entries are means. Statistical significance based on two-tailed difference in means *t*-test.

On the other hand, when taking into consideration individual preferences – how respondents felt about the particular issue – systematic changes should emerge. Those who initially agreed with the position the Court adopted should show an increase in *support for the Court*. Those who disagreed should show a decrease in *support for the Court*. In other words, change in *support for the Court* should be at least partially driven by *support for the policy*. Thus the first hypothesis to test is as follows:

Change in Support for the Court Hypothesis: *Those who initially agree (disagree) with the position the Court adopts should show an increase (decrease) in support for the Court.*

In other words, if Court decisions do matter as an ingredient in support for the Court, there should be a relationship between *support for the Court* and *support for the policy*. Simple correlations between support for the issue and support for the court – shown in Table 5-3 – are a straightforward first look at the relationship. Both of these variables are measured using seven-point scales where (1) indicates "very strongly disapprove" of both the Court and the position the Court ultimately takes, and (7) indicates "very strongly approve"of both. These two variables should be positively correlated. Included are both the first- and second-wave measures of *support for the Court*. Of greater interest are the results from the second wave, however, since this tells more about the effect of the specific decision in question on attitudes toward the Court. At the first wave, the respondents

TABLE 5-3. *Relationship between Support for the Supreme Court and Policy Agreement*

	Center Moriches	Monroe	Oklahoma	Oregon
First Wave	−.25**	.08	.00	.27*
	(.01)	(.22)	(.49)	(.02)
Second Wave	–	.27**	.11	.26*
		(.01)	(.31)	(.02)
N	93	88	24	59

Note: Cell entries are correlation coefficients. Probability values are in parentheses. ** $p <$ .01, * $p < .05$, one-tailed hypothesis test.

obviously did not know how the Court would decide the case, so this information reveals little about the effect of the decision.

Table 5-3 shows that there is some evidence of a connection between these two variables. In two of the four studies, there was a significant correlation between *support for the policy* and *support for the Court* before it handed down its decision. This, however, does not explain much about the effect of the actual decision on support. The second-wave measures are more informative. They point out that in two of the three studies that included *support for the Court* in the second wave, there was indeed a positive and significant relationship between *support for the policy* and *support for the Court*. Only among the Monroe respondents is the second wave different from the first. Prior to the decision there was no relationship between how respondents felt about the school district and how they felt about the Court. After the Court ruled, a distinct relationship emerged. This supports the idea that respondents updated their beliefs about the Court. In the Oklahoma study, there appeared to be no relationship either before or after the Court's decision, which suggests very little to no updating of beliefs. In the Oregon study, the relationship existed both before and after the decision, which makes it unclear whether or not there was any updating of information. The evidence thus far is not resounding.

But, the expectation was not for the Court's decision to affect all of the respondents equally. Instead, the connection should be stronger for those from the immediate community than among those from the surrounding communities. As demonstrated by the results in Chapter 3, those from the immediate community should find the case to be more important, and therefore should also give greater emphasis to the decision than those from the surrounding communities. That leads to the following hypothesis:

TABLE 5-4. *Relationship between Support for the Supreme Court and Policy Agreement by Geographic Community*

	Center Moriches	Monroe	Oklahoma	Oregon
Immediate Community				
First Wave	−.04	.23	.08	.25
	(.38)	(.08)	(.38)	(.07)
Second Wave	−	.51**	.02	43**
		(.00)	(.47)	(.01)
N	57	40	16	35
Surrounding Community				
First Wave	−.44**	−.06	−.46	.11
	(.00)	(.35)	(.13)	(.31)
Second Wave	−	.03	.31	.01
		(.41)	(.23)	(.49)
N	36	48	8	24

Note: Cell entries are correlation coefficients. Probability values are in parentheses. ** $p <$ .01,* $p < $ .05, one-tailed hypothesis test.

Town of Residence/Support for the Court Hypothesis: The effect of policy agreement on support for the Court should be conditioned on town of residence. Those from the immediate community should attach greater significance to the decision, and thus show greater change according to how they initially felt about the issue.

To uncover whether there is any evidence to support this hypothesis, an analysis of support for the Court and support for the policy is again done, but this time is further differentiated by town of residence. The results are shown in Table 5-4.

Table 5-4 provides a much more vivid picture of the connection between *support for the policy* and *support for the Court*. Looking first at those from the immediate community (the top half of the table), as expected prior to the Court's ruling, there was no connection between *support for the Court* at the first wave and *support for the policy* at the first wave. However, once it handed down its decision, there was a much stronger connection – in fact a statistically significant one in two of the studies – between *support for the policy* and *support for the Court*. It is worth noting again that the relationship in the Monroe and Oregon studies changed among people from the immediate communities, who generally felt more strongly about the issue than those from the surrounding communities.

In the lower half of the table, which displays the results for those who reside in the surrounding communities, there was no evidence of a relationship between *support for the Court* and *support for the policy*. The only instance of a statistically significant effect was in the first wave of the Center Moriches study, but it was a negative one.

The results, thus far, lend some support for the hypothesis that those from the immediate communities were making connections between the support for how the Court decides the case and support for the Court itself. There is very little evidence, though, that the same is true for those from the surrounding communities. However, there may still be other ways in which the Court's decision might affect its level of support.

The final connection yet to be explored before presenting the multivariate results is the relationship between *support for the policy* and *support for the Court* based on the respondent's level of education. One reason for the weak results thus far may be that some people simply have more informed opinions about the Court than other individuals. Those whose views of the Court are based on knowledge of many Court decisions are simply less likely to change their opinion drastically in response to a single decision than someone with less information. People with less information may be less confident in their assessment of the Court; and, what scant information they have may be outdated compared with that of their more informed counterparts. This is consistent with Franklin and Kosaki's (1995) findings. Their research found that those with more prior information about the Court were more likely to have opinions toward the Court that reflected the actual ideological tenor of Court decisions.

Since education is a good predictor of such knowledge (see Chapter 3), those with less education, and hence less information about the Court, should be most influenced by a single Court decision. Those with higher levels of education should be less influenced by a single Court decision, since they already have informed opinions about the Court. To test this relationship, it is necessary to examine the correlation between *support for the policy* and *support for the Court* by different levels of education. This leads to the following final hypothesis in this chapter:

Education/Policy Agreement/Support for the Court Hypothesis: *Those with more education should be less affected by the Court's decision than those with less education.*

Education is measured using five categories: (1) less than high school, (2) high school, (3) some college, (4) college degree, and (5) post-graduate education. Only those who knew about the Court's decision were included in the analysis. Because this left so few people in some of the categories, the respondents from the Monroe, Oregon, and Oklahoma studies are

TABLE 5-5. *Relationship between Support for the Supreme Court and Policy Agreement by Level of Education among those who knew about the Decision*

	Less Than High School	High School	Some College	College Degree	Post-Graduate Education
	.56	.27*	.48**	.18	.09
$p=$	.16	.03	.00	.17	.30
N	5	51	46	31	38

Note: Entries are correlation coefficients. ** $p < .01$, * $p < .05$. Probabilities are based on one-tailed significance tests.

grouped together. (There was no second-wave measure of support for the Court in the Center Moriches study.) The results are presented in Table 5-5.

Table 5-5 shows that there is indeed a stronger connection between the individual's *support for the policy* and subsequent *support for the Court* – an effect that appears highly contingent upon *education*. The connection between support for the policy position and support for the Court is significantly greater among the less educated respondents in the sample than it is for the better educated. For those with less than a high school education, the correlation is .56 ($p = .16$). Although, it does not quite reach standard levels of statistical significance due to the sample size (N = 5), it approaches significance and is substantively strong. Among those with a high school diploma, the relationship is positive (.27) and statistically significant ($p = .03$). It is also significant among those with some college (.48, $p < .00$). However, among those with at least a college education, the effect disappears. Why? Those with greater education should be less affected by a single Court decision. They are more knowledgeable, and thus, more likely to have heard about other decisions. Those with less education, and hence less knowledge, are much more easily influenced. A single decision may overwhelm their attitude. This is consistent with results reported by Franklin and Kosaki (1995).

To test for any spurious effects, this exact same relationship is examined among those who had not heard of the Court's decision. Since these respondents had not heard about the decision, there should be no relationship – regardless of their level of education – between how they felt about the issue and how they felt about the Court. Those results, presented in Table 5-6, are not significant for any of the groups. They come close to reaching statistical significance among those with some college ($p = .09$) but the relationship is negative.

TABLE 5-6. *Relationship between Support for the Supreme Court and Policy Agreement by Level of Education among those who did not know about the Decision*

	Less Than High School	High School	Some College	College Degree	Post-Graduate Education
	.11	−.02	−.17	.02	−.26
$p=$	.34	.43	.09	.44	.10
N	17	64	62	41	25

Note: Entries are correlation coefficients. Probabilities are based on one-tailed significance tests. ** $p < .01$, * $p < .05$.

The Multivariate Analysis of Individual-Level Support for the Court

The results from the preliminary analyses provide initial evidence that Court decisions may be important ingredients in support for the Court – especially when considering town of residence and level of education. The patterns were not uniform, however, and these relatively simple analyses do not include many controls. Since the data were not collected as part of a true experiment – with individuals randomly assigned to different conditions – controlling for the effects of other variables becomes especially important. What is needed is a multivariate model that simultaneously examines the role the independent variables play on change in support for the Court while controlling for each of the other variables.

To estimate such a model, a dependent variable is needed to measure change in support for the Court. This is created by simply subtracting the respondent's evaluation of the Court offered at the first wave from the evaluation offered at the second wave. Evaluation of the Court is measured by simply asking people whether they approve or disapprove of the Court, followed by a question that asks how strongly they approve or disapprove. Responses to these questions are combined into a simple seven-point, Likert-type scale. The scales used to create the dependent variable are the same scales analyzed above. The dependent variable is calculated such that positive values indicate an increase in support for the Court following the decision, and negative values indicate a less favorable evaluation of the Court.

Four independent variables are included in the analysis.[4] First is a measure of the *initial evaluation of the Court*, which ranges from −3

---

[4] The analysis presented also appears in Hoekstra (2000). The only difference is in the coding of the variables. Previously, prior support for the Court and prior opinion on the

(disapprove very strongly) to +3 (approve very strongly). This variable is included in order to control for any regression effects, which is the tendency for extreme values to become less extreme on subsequent measurements (Markus 1990; Finkel 1995). Since initial values may be negatively related to subsequent values, the coefficient should be negative. The estimate is also of substantive importance. A simple transformation of the coefficient $(1 + \beta)$ provides information on the more substantive interpretation. The number that results from this transformation is exactly the same as the effect of prior level of support on current levels of support (Finkel 1995). For example, with the dependent variable measured as change, the prior evaluation coefficient was estimated to be $-.35$, which shows that some portion of the change is due to stability in support for the Court $(1 + [-.35] = .65)$. In other words, about 65 percent of the current support of the Court is explained by prior support. Since the conventional wisdom is that the Court is insulated from the effect of its decisions, the more cautious approach is to include prior evaluation in the specification.

The second independent variable is the respondent's *initial opinion on the issue*. This is also measured on a seven-point scale where -3 indicates that the respondent "very strongly disagreed" initially with the position that the Court ultimately adopted, and $+3$ indicates that the respondent "very strongly agreed" with the position the Court adopted. The resulting coefficient should be positive if Court decisions factor into support.

The third variable is *town of residence*. It is coded (1) for those who reside in the immediate community and (0) for those who reside elsewhere. This coding is exactly the opposite from how it was coded in the previous chapter. Recall that in Chapter 4's examination of opinion change on the issue, those from the surrounding communities should exhibit the greatest amount of change; but, here the expectation is exactly the opposite. In Chapter 3, residents in the immediate community generally rated the issues in the cases as more important than did those from the surrounding communities. Since they feel more strongly about the issue than their more geographically removed counterparts, the effect of the decision should be more pronounced among the immediate community respondents. This expectation is bolstered by the results presented in the previous tables. However, since the effect of *town of*

issue were measured on seven-point scales; however, instead of ranging from −3 to +3, the coding was from 1 to 7. Therefore some of the numbers in the table appear different, but the substantive interpretation is the same.

TABLE 5-7. *Change in Support for the Supreme Court*

	Monroe	Oklahoma	Oregon
Initial Evaluation of Court	−.23**	−.25	−.47**
	(.09)	(.16)	(.12)
Initial Opinion on Issue	.07	.51*	−.03
	(.09)	(.26)	(.13)
Town of Residence	−.26	.01	.58
	(.29)	(.60)	(.54)
Initial Opinion*Town of Residence	.20*	−.54*	.37*
	(.12)	(.28)	(.20)
Constant	.10	.46	.05
	(.23)	(.50)	(.36)
$F =$	3.89	2.18	4.72
Probability of $F =$	.01	.11	.00
Adjusted $R^2 =$	.12	.17	.20
N	88	24	59

Note: The measure of support for the Court was not included on the second wave of the Center Moriches study. $* p < .05$, $** p < .01$, one-tailed hypothesis test. Standard errors are in parentheses.

residence is conditioned upon *initial opinion on the issue*, there is no expectation for the direction of this variable as a main effect. The effect of *town of residence* should emerge when interacted with respondent's *initial opinion on the issue* (*initial opinion*town of residence*). This interaction, and its individual components, tests whether the effect of agreement or disagreement is greater among those from the immediate community than among those from the surrounding communities.[5] The results are presented in Table 5-7.[6] The first thing to note is that *initial evaluation of the Court* proves significant in two of the three studies (Monroe and Oregon). Prior attitudes spilling over into current evaluations of the Court are consistent with the results of previous research. In Monroe, the coefficient of −.23 suggests that about 77 percent (1 + [−.23]) of prior evaluation explains current evaluation. In Oregon, about 53 percent is explained by

[5] In the multivariate analysis, education is not included. Education does not prove statistically significant in the multivariate models and does not alter the statistical significance or substance of the other independent variables. It is excluded because of the relatively small sample size and small number of respondents in some of the education categories.

[6] Again, because the coding of the variables is different than in previous publications (Hoekstra 2000), the coefficients in the table appear somewhat different. However, the substantive interpretation, presented here in Table 5-8, is exactly the same.

TABLE 5-8. *Predicted Change in Support for the Supreme Court*

	Initial Opinion on the Issue = 1 Initial Evaluation of Court = −1		Initial Opinion on the Issue = −1 Initial Evaluation of Court = 1	
	Immediate Community	Surrounding Community	Immediate Community	Surrounding Community
Monroe	.34	.40	−.66	−.20
Oklahoma	.69	1.22	.25	−.3
Oregon	1.44	.49	−.18	−.39
	Initial Opinion on the Issue = 2 Initial Evaluation of Court = −2		Initial Opinion on the Issue = −2 Initial Evaluation of Court = 2	
	Immediate Community	Surrounding Community	Immediate Community	Surrounding Community
Monroe	.84	.70	−1.16	−.50
Oklahoma	.91	1.98	.03	−1.06
Oregon	2.25	.93	−.99	−.83
	Initial Opinion on the Issue = 3 Initial Evaluation of Court = −3		Initial Opinion on the Issue = −3 Initial Evaluation of Court = 3	
	Immediate Community	Surrounding Community	Immediate Community	Surrounding Community
Monroe	1.34	1.00	−1.66	−.80
Oklahoma	1.13	2.74	−.19	−1.82
Oregon	3.06	1.37	−1.80	−1.27

prior evaluation of the Court. In Oklahoma, however, the coefficient is not statistically significant.

At the same time, prior attitudes do not explain all of the change. The Court's decisions do indeed alter feelings about the Court, as suggested by the interaction between *town of residence* and *initial opinion*. The coefficient is significant in all three studies. It is positive, as predicted, in two of the studies (Monroe and Oregon), but it is negatively signed in the Oklahoma study. Because of the interaction, it is difficult to interpret the substantive effect of these variables by just looking at the coefficients in the table. To ease the substantive explanation of this analysis, Table 5-8 presents predicted values.

The entries in Table 5-8 are derived from varying the values of three variables: *town of residence, initial opinion on the issue,* and *initial evaluation of the court.* Recall that the hypothesis predicted that, overall, agreement or disagreement with the Court's decision should affect how people subsequently felt about the Court. Moreover, this effect was expected to be magnified among the residents of the immediate communities. (reflected in the interaction between *initial opinion* and *town of residence*). In terms of this table, the absolute value of the predicted values should be greater among the residents of the immediate community. The left half of the table represents the predicted values for those who initially *agreed* with the position the Court ultimately takes, but who previously *disapproved* of the Court. The predicted values in these columns should be positive since the Court agrees with the respondent and the Court has room to improve in the respondent's eyes. The columns on the right show the opposite effects: the predicted values for those who initially *disagreed* with how the Court ultimately decided, but who previously *approved* of the Court. The values in these columns should be negative since respondents should be disappointed with the Court for announcing a decision they dislike. Moving down the table, the magnitude of the difference between initial support for the Court and initial support for the issue increases, so the absolute predicted values should increase as well.

The expected pattern comes through crisply, especially in the Monroe and Oregon cases. For example, looking at the predicted change in support for the Court among those who initially strongly agreed with how the Court decided (initial opinion = 2) but who had previously strongly disapproved of the Court (initial evaluation = −2), the model predicts that everyone becomes more favorable toward the Supreme Court. In Monroe and Oregon, the increase was greater among those from the immediate community, precisely as expected. In the Oklahoma study, however, the residents of the surrounding communities showed greater change in support. Nevertheless, each group did change in the predicted direction.

The same pattern is found by looking at those who disagreed with the Court's ultimate decision (initial opinion = −2), but who previously approved of the Court (initial evaluation of Court = 2). Except in one instance (the residents of the immediate community in Oklahoma), everyone is predicted to become less supportive of the Court. The amount of change varies in each study. Those in the immediate community in the Oklahoma study actually showed a positive, but negligible, increase in support (.03). But those from the immediate community in Monroe showed more than one full point decrease in support for the Court (−1.16). Since the measure of support is only a seven-point scale, a change of that magnitude is substantively important.

The largest predicted changes are in the lowest third of the table. These entries are the predicted values when opinion on the issue and attitude toward the Court were most in discord. These are the people who very strongly disapproved of the Court (-3) but who also very strongly approved of the Court's ultimate decision (3), and vice versa. It is not surprising that the greatest change was evident among those individuals.[7]

What Table 5-8 does is dramatically show how geographic proximity, policy agreement, and prior support for the Court affect changes in support for that institution in the wake of its actions. In all three studies, the results clearly support that hearing about a decision affects how people view the Court. Furthermore, there was consistent evidence that this effect was contingent upon how strongly one feels about the issue (here measured as geographic proximity). Although this effect was only in the predicted direction for two of the three studies included in this analysis, the substantive effect came through clearly. In the third study, Oklahoma, there was evidence of an overall effect of agreement or disagreement with the Court's decisions, but this effect was actually most pronounced among the residents of the surrounding community rather than immediate community. Nonetheless, policy agreement was an important part of subsequent support.

CONCLUSION AND DISCUSSION

Court decisions matter. Using individual level data provides more clear and convincing evidence that satisfaction with those decisions influences subsequent evaluations of the Court. This is something that aggregate data have had difficulty uncovering. This is not to say that evaluations of the Court are based *solely* on satisfaction with Court decisions, only that decisions are also an ingredient in individual levels of support. Surely, the effect of an unpopular decision is mitigated, to some extent, by perceptions that the Court operates in a less political, partisan, or ideological fashion, as the process argument suggests (Hibbing and Theiss-Morse 1995), or by a commitment to democratic values, as Caldeira and Gibson (1992) argue.

The dynamic argument, suggested by other scholars, is also supported by the data (Caldeira and Gibson 1992; Mondak and Smithey 1997). Prior evaluations of the Court carry over into subsequent evaluations after hearing about specific Court decisions. However, the critical point of the analysis is that public reactions to Court decisions are clearly important – much more so than previously recognized. This is not to say that Court

---

[7] Since this bottom third of the table contains some out of sample predictions, the predicted values should be interpreted cautiously.

decisions have an immediate effect on the Court's institutional legitimacy as scholars such as Caldeira and Gibson (1992) conceptualize and measure it. It is extremely unlikely that one poorly received decision would lead to calls for fundamental changes to the Court's powers, which is how diffuse support is measured in Caldeira and Gibson's work. However, it is clear that one decision can alter *confidence in*, or *support for* the institution. This is not a trivial matter. This change in confidence or support could greatly help or hinder implementation of the decision in the same way that a president's popularity can increase or decrease his persuasive appeal. Or, quite possibly, a series of poorly received decisions might actually lead to calls for institutional changes, which might even be reflected in diffuse support as Caldeira and Gibson measure it. At the very least, Chief Justice Rehnquist's concerns expressed at the outset of this chapter may be well founded. If public trust and confidence in courts are related to the decisions they make, judicial independence may be a difficult ideal to maintain.

Are these results enduring? With the data included in this study, it is difficult to know with a great deal of certainty. Since the second wave of the study took place shortly after the Court handed down its decision, it is impossible to know whether the effects are lasting ones. However, a great deal of research in political psychology supports the argument that the effects may not be fleeting. For example, in their work on on-line information processing, Lodge, McGraw, and Stroh (1989, see also Lodge, Steenbergen, and Brau 1995) find that people incorporate new pieces of information into an existing impression, or running tally. The impression of a political actor is updated as new information is encountered and processed. However, specific details about those individual bits of information may not be easily recalled at a future date. This research suggests that when citizens heard about the Court's decision, they reevaluated how they felt about the Court and stored these updated impressions. However, if the same respondents were asked about the Court decision at some later date, they may not be able to recall specific information, even if it did influence their current assessment of the Court.

The long-term implications of these results are consistent with Franklin and Kosaki's (1995) finding that those with greater levels of education are less likely to be influenced by additional information about the Court. In theory, those with more education are likely to express opinions regarding the Court based on larger stores of information – making it less likely for a single decision to have a huge effect. But, it is unlikely that any new information about the Court will overwhelm existing attitudes or that the effect of one decision cannot be overcome with subsequent decisions. According to Mondak and Smithey (1997), the Court can, over time, regenerate public support.

What does this mean for the Court? Though levels of support for the Court tend to be higher than levels of support for the other branches of government, it is difficult to determine the underlying individual level explanation using aggregate data, as individual patterns may be hidden (see also Mondak and Smithey 1997). Each of the studies presented here elicited neither uniform support nor resounding opposition to the Court's decision. Some people were pleased with the Court's decision and expressed more favorable evaluations of the Court, whereas others were not pleased and expressed less favorable opinions. As with public opinion in general, views on these issues were divided.

6

Conclusion

Balancing Independence and Support

LOCAL MEDIA COVERAGE

What is the nature of the relationship between the Supreme Court and public opinion? Obviously, it is a complicated one. The Supreme Court makes decisions on some of the most complex and salient issues of the day. They also resolve more routine policy questions. To some degree they are able to do so with less intense media and public scrutiny than Congress or the executive branch. But, as the results from these studies show, the institution is by no means removed from the public eye. The media, especially the local media, pay a great deal of attention to the Court – much more than previously recognized. Looking at national coverage of Court cases overlooks the simple fact that not all cases are equally newsworthy to all citizens in all media markets. If the results from this book point to anything, it is that the local media were much more likely to provide consumers with information on homegrown cases than were the national media or the media from other parts of the nation.

As detailed in Chapter 3, the local media provided both quantity and quality of coverage. Even *The New York Times*, this nation's paper of record, did not do a better job than the local media. The local newspapers devoted more space than did other newspapers. But, more than that, the local papers often started covering the cases at a much earlier stage, beginning with the initial dispute in the lower courts and sustaining the coverage as the cases moved through the courts. They included the Supreme Court's decision to grant certiorari, the presentation of oral arguments, and finally, the coverage of the Court's decision. The local media also reported extensively once the decision was announced – providing information on the background of the dispute, the Court's decision and reasoning, and sometimes even the separate opinions. In some instances, the newspapers continued to cover these issues even after the state legislatures responded to the Court's decision.

That being said, there were differences in coverage between the cases. In particular, the Monroe case involving the creation of a special school district for the disabled Hasidic school children received a great deal of media attention. This controversy involved a very visible local group that had been at the center of many previous controversies. Thus, the extensive coverage of the case – including the Court's decision – was not all that surprising. In the Oregon case, both the local and national media payed significant attention to the general dispute between environmentalists and the logging industry over government regulations to protect the spotted owl. This has been and continues to be one of the most important issues in the Pacific Northwest over the last few decades. However, much of the media coverage did not focus on this specific case. Throughout this controversy, local media attention was much more extensive than national media attention. Any controversy over the spotted owl is more likely to be newsworthy near the owl's natural habitat than in other parts of the country.

But even less controversial cases received substantial coverage. In particular, the Center Moriches cases, involving an otherwise innocuous local church and its request to use the high school auditorium to show a film, generated extensive local coverage. The other civil liberties case (Monroe) received significant – though not as thorough – attention. Although economic disputes are sometimes overlooked by the mainstream media, the Oklahoma tax case received substantial coverage in the local media.

This extensive local coverage makes sense since local reporters are most familiar with their communities and the local issues. These local reporters are also much more likely to have access to community leaders and the parties involved in the dispute. But the most important reason for local papers to cover these stories is simply that their readers are much more likely to be interested.

Extensions of the Geographic Argument

Are these effects limited to the local media and the local geographic communities that they serve? Not necessarily. Not all forms of media are geographically defined. There are national newspapers, national news magazines, professional journals and newsletters, associational magazines, as well as ever-increasing forms of electronic information, to name just a few. Virtually every professional group has an association newsletter, a point emphasized by Berkson's research (1978) that reports extensive knowledge of cases relevant to one's occupation.

It is impossible for many communities to have a case before the Supreme Court each term. However, most local papers nationwide are likely to cover many of the Supreme Court cases. Instead of focusing only on national or local, research needs to broaden the focus to include regional, professional, and religious groups, to name just a few possibilities. There are other options of how and where to look for information about Supreme Court decisions among members of the mass public. To some extent, the decision to look at geographic communities has been a way to test a more general theoretical argument about access to, and interest in, Supreme Court cases. However, due to the geographic nature of most media markets, these effects are probably most obvious and easy to uncover in and around the local communities where these coventroversies began. But, these effects are certainly not limited to the local communities, especially as the ways in which people receive information continue to evolve.

LOCAL AWARENESS OF THE CASES

The stage was clearly set for Court decisions to affect public opinion in these local communities. Many residents took advantage of the extensive local media coverage to learn about the case. Not surprisingly, public attention and interest coincided with media attention. Although not perfectly correlated, the more extensive the media coverage, the greater the knowledge. The predecision coverage – from the onset of the conflict, through lower court battles, until the time the Court accepted the case for review and oral arguments – was important in attracting local interest and helped create a sense of anticipation among community members. Citizens not only knew about, but also cared about, the Court's decisions.

Importantly, knowledge and interest were generally higher in the immediate communities than in the surrounding communities, even though access to information was basically constant. This finding is consistent with research from social psychology that suggests that individuals may come to identify with similarly situated people (Boninger, et al. 1995). The intense interest and widespread information contradict the conventional wisdom portraying the public as largely ignorant of information about the Court. Those with a closer connection to the case, measured here in terms of geography, were more likely to hear about the decision than were those with a more remote connection, despite similar access to information. So, members of the general communities (i.e., both the immediate and surrounding) were much more likely to hear about these local cases than were people who reside elsewhere in the nation; and, those from the immediate community were often – though not always – more likely to hear about these cases than were members of surrounding communities. The closer residents lived to the case's place of origin, the more likely they were to have an interest in and to learn about that Supreme Court case.

Other factors influenced attention to Supreme Court cases. Individuals who closely follow politics and the media in general, and those with higher levels of education, were more likely to pay attention to the cases. The unique data collected for this book were able to provide information on how individual characteristics such as education, attention to politics, and geographic proximity increase awareness of Court decisions. That kind of information is not easily obtained in national studies where access to information varies so widely. Specifically, by looking in these local communities where the supply of information is constant, it was possible to examine precisely the effect of these individual level factors on knowledge of the Court. The results from the geographic samples suggest that access to information is indeed critical; but, while some individuals are merely passive recipients of information, many others prefer to seek out information. Motivation was as important as access.

So, with these four studies, it was possible to accomplish two tasks: to examine how media coverage affects awareness by linking coverage within these communities with aggregate levels of awareness, and to examine how individual level factors – geographic proximity, education, attention to politics, attention to the media, and others – affect awareness by looking *within* the samples where access to information was constant. This is something that national studies simply cannot do.

THE SUPREME COURT AND THE LEGITIMATION HYPOTHESIS

What happens when people learn about a Court decision? Does it affect how they feel about the issue? Chapter 4 showed there was only slight evidence that the Court can shape public opinion on the issues. In two of the four studies there was some evidence of opinion change in the direction of the Court's decision. However, it was difficult to explain this change. Unlike what the persuasion research would expect, shifts in opinion, whether positive or negative, were not related to support for the Court. Normally, support for the Court – or any other source of a message – should positively affect how people feel about the issue. Those who have a great deal of confidence in the Court should be more likely to be persuaded than those with less confidence. This is also what some experimental studies have shown (Mondak 1990, 1992, 1994; Hoekstra 1995). This was not the case, however.

While the results for the persuasive appeal of the Court were less than overwhelming, there was some evidence to suggest that the frequency with which people pay attention to politics and the media, thereby increasing their exposure to information about the Court's decisions, increased the Court's ability to persuade. This finding was limited to two of the four studies, however. In some respects these findings are consistent with previous research that shows very little aggregate opinion shifts (Marshall 1988, 1989). On the other hand, there is some recent research suggesting Court decisions have the potential to polarize opinion (Franklin and Kosaki 1989; Johnson and Martin 1998). However, that research was limited to highly controversial issues such as abortion and the death penalty. Not too surprisingly then, there was no evidence of polarization following these four cases. These cases simply were not as charged as issues such as abortion and capital punishment.

Most surprising was the fact that the null findings were also inconsistent with experimental research, which has provided the strongest evidence to date that the Supreme Court might be able to influence attitudes – at least on some issues (Hoekstra 1995) and under certain conditions (Mondak 1991). One possibility is that while the media covered these cases extensively, it may not have been extensive enough to reach those who are most likely to be persuaded by the Court's decision – those with less ability to counterargue. In the laboratory, acquisition of information is a less onerous task as the experiment typically provides participants with information and eliminates most distractions. The experimental results that suggest the Court's *potential* to persuade cannot be dismissed. In fact, the laboratory may be the best option for further development of hypotheses to test in the "real world."

Another potential explanation for the null results is the lack of variability in *support for the Court* and *opinion change* among the respondents. Most people expressed a great deal of confidence in the Court; however, very few people exhibited much opinion change. Thus, there was little to work with statistically.

While this statistical explanation might be accurate, we cannot overlook the possibility that the Court simply does not act as a persuasive political actor. This is consistent with much of the survey research but inconsistent with the results of some experimental work. What future research needs to explore in greater detail is whether the results from experimental studies are driven by artifacts of the research process. First, does the use of college students as the subjects affect the results? Quite possibly, this group is more prone to persuasion from the Court than the typical citizen would be (Sears 1986), which could explain the differences often noted between experimental and survey research.

Second, does the timing matter when measuring opinion change? In the experimental setting, subjects' attitudes are usually measured in a very short span of time. Once they read about a Court decision, they are then immediately asked to rate how they feel about the issue. In the typical survey context, it might be months or even years between exposure to a Court case and measurement of the respondents' attitudes (Mondak and Smithey 1997). This is one explanation for the differences often found between experimental and survey research. Although first-wave subjects in this study were contacted within two weeks of the Court's decisions, it is quite possible that this lapse was long enough for any persuasive effect to disappear. If so, this does not bode well for the Court. If persuasion aids implementation, then implementation would have to occur immediately. It is highly unlikely that decisions could be implemented in such a short span of time.

Further research might be able to differentiate between these explanations by using a more diverse group of subjects, by varying the time between measurements, and by devising questions that capture additional differences in the key variables. Despite using close to an ideal research design, this research did not clearly demonstrate evidence of the Court's persuasiveness.

The implications are critically important to understanding the Supreme Court. Since the Court lacks the power of the purse and the sword, it must often rely on public acceptance – frequently, local acceptance – for implementation of its decisions. It is not clear whether the Court's political capital can assist in that implementation. Does this mean that the Court must consider prevailing opinion when deciding whether to accept cases and how to decide these cases? The answer is a definitive maybe.

Recent research on the role of public opinion on Supreme Court decision making is equally ambiguous. Some research finds that the justices respond to public opinion, but such effects are typically very small and limited to a handful of justices (Mishler and Sheehan 1993, 1996; Stimson, et al. 1995; Flemming and Wood 1997). Other research finds no such effects (Norpoth and Segal 1994). It is possible that this research relies on the wrong measure of public opinion – usually *national* public opinion – when examining this question. Alternatively, the justices may simply forgo the opportunity to hear a case where public acceptance is critical to implementation, but where they perceive that opposition is likely to be high.

LIMITED POLITICAL CAPITAL?

While there was only scant and inconsistent evidence within these studies that the Court can change attitudes on the issues involved in the cases, there was stronger and more consistent evidence that these decisions can factor into support for the Court. On average, individuals who initially supported the policy that the Court ultimately adopted as their decision became more supportive of the Court. Those who opposed at the outset became less supportive. In two of the three studies that measured support for the Court at both waves, these effects were stronger among those from the immediate community than those from the surrounding communities. Consistent with the *Town of Residence/Support for the Court Hypothesis*, the immediate community generally attached greater policy relevance to the case than did those from the surrounding communities, especially when asked how important they thought the issue was to their communities.

There was also some evidence that residents with lower levels of education were swayed more by this new information than those with higher levels of education. Similar to Franklin and Kosaki's (1995) findings, it seems individuals with more education have larger stores of political information. Their opinion of the Court may be formed from a wider scope of information; therefore, a single decision is less likely to change their feelings about the Court. The extensive local media coverage of these cases may have been sufficient to reach those with less education and knowledge of the Court – those most likely to reevaluate their evaluation of the Court. This finding was consistent with the *Education/Policy Agreement/Support for the Court Hypothesis*.

Most of the previous accounts of support for the Court are skeptical about the role that decisions play in public evaluations of the Court. Instead, they argue that the public has too little information to use, or that even with information, evaluations are based on other criteria, such as how the Court conducts its business or commitment to democratic values. The findings presented in Chapter 5 shed new light on this research question. Although decisions do factor into the equation, they are not the only ingredient, and may not even be the main ingredient. Also, it is not likely that these more short-term influences will override long-term levels of support. If the Court loses some support as the result of unpopular decisions, it can probably make up for negative reactions (Mondak and Smithey 1997). People's feelings about the Court are not created with each decision, but are updated as they encounter new and relevant information. If there is some inertia to the process, as Chapter 5 suggests, and prior opinion carries over into current opinion, what makes up the prior opinion? Is it the cumulative effect of prior decisions? Is it due to how the Court operates? Is it commitment to Democratic values? Is it a mixture of these factors? This remains to be answered.

Research that suggests the Court benefits from positive public perceptions of how it conducts its business is undoubtedly correct. While the results from Chapter 4 suggest – albeit not strongly – that extensive coverage of the Court's decisions might increase acceptance, the Court probably also benefits from less intense media and public scrutiny of the inner workings of the institution than the other branches of government. The Court itself must know this as they continue to guard the secrecy of their deliberations and the many institutional norms that keep it in place. But, it is important not to discount the role of policy in public evaluations of that institution. The research here suggests that it plays a role. Like any other institution, support for the Court is made up of more than a single ingredient. Evaluations based on policy and process are not mutually exclusive.

As scholars of American political institutions, instead of striving for separate theories of support for the various government institutions, it is better to strive for common theories that account for differences. Although these institutions display individual characteristics, they also share important features. Each institution is driven by policy concerns. The Supreme Court may not be motivated by electoral concerns; however, like Congress and the executive branch, the Supreme Court relies heavily on public support and links that support to the decisions it makes.

Appendix A

Sampling

The initial sampling frame for the Center Moriches study included 326 working telephone numbers. Of these 326 numbers, 212 were contacted and agreed to participate in the first wave of the study, for a response rate of 65 percent. Of these 212 initial respondents, 112 were successfully recontacted and agreed to participate in the second wave, for a retention rate of 52.8 percent.

For the Monroe study, 167 respondents (from a sampling frame of 300 working numbers) were contacted and agreed to participate in the first wave, for a response rate of 55.67 percent. Of these 167 respondents, 122 were successfully recontacted and agreed to participate in the second wave, for a retention rate of 73.1 percent.

In the Oklahoma study, 206 people participated in the first wave. The initial sampling frame consisted of 395, for a response rate of 52.15 percent. The second wave successfully recontacted 116 of the 206 initial respondents, for a retention rate of 56.3 percent.

In the Oregon study, the initial sampling frame included 413 phone numbers. Of these, 243 people were contacted, for a response rate of 58.8 percent. For the second wave, 145 were contacted and agreed to participate, for a retention rate of 59.7 percent.

Overall, 836 individuals participated in the first wave; and, of these, 495 respondents were contacted following the Court's decision and agreed to be interviewed again.

Appendix B

Survey Instruments Included in the Analysis

How many days in the past week did you watch the news on TV?

How many days in the last week did you read a daily newspaper?

How many days in the last week did you discuss politics with friends or family members?

Next, I'd like to ask your opinion on a few issues being discussed in the news lately. We understand that most people may not have the time or interest to follow every issue in the news. However, we are interested in knowing how you feel about a few of these issues, how much time you spend thinking about these issues, and how important they are to you.

Center Moriches: Do you feel that a religious group ought to be allowed to use public school facilities after school hours if other community groups are allowed to use the facilities, or do you believe that a church should not be allowed to use the school facilities?

Monroe: Do you believe that it is all right for school districts to be specially created for a community sharing a common religious faith, or do you believe that there should not be special consideration of religious beliefs when creating school districts?

Oklahoma: Do you think Oklahoma's gasoline tax should be collected on gasoline sold by Native Americans on tribal land, or do you think the government should not be involved in tribal business?

Oregon: Do you think the government should protect the habitat of endangered species with strict building restrictions? Or, do you think the government goes too far in protecting endangered species?

After the issue-specific questions, these four follow-up questions were asked:

Do you hold this opinion very strongly, strongly, or not so strongly?

Compared to other issues you might think about, how much time do you spend thinking about this sort of issue? Would you say you think about it a lot of the time, some of the time, or not much of the time?

Compared to other issues you might think about, how important do you think this issue is to you personally? Would you say it is very important, somewhat important, or not very important?

Compared to other issues you might think about, how important do you think this issue is to your community? Would you say it is very important, somewhat important, or not very important?

Now let's consider the way the U.S. Supreme Court makes decisions. I'm going to read you a series of statements. . . .

In general do you approve or disapprove of the way the Supreme Court is handling its job?

Do you approve/disapprove very strongly, strongly or not strongly?

What is the highest grade of school or year of college you have completed?

What town do you live in?

We understand that most people may not have the time or the interest to follow everything that happens in the news. However we are interested in knowing whether or not you have read or heard anything in the news recently about the issue of (issue in case)? (If yes, asked to explain)

(if they mention the Supreme Court) And how did the Supreme Court decide?

Appendix C

Local and National Media Coverage of a Sample of Supreme Court Cases: 1996–97 Term

Case	Local media stories		The New York Times
1. *Arkansas v. Farm Credit Services of Central Arkansas*	1	*Arkansas Democrat Gazette*	0
2. *Atherton v. FDIC*	1	*The Star-Ledger*	0
3. *Bennett v. Spear*	2	*The Bulletin*	2
4. *Board of the County Commissioners of Bryan County, Oklahoma v. Brown*	1(1)	*The Daily Oklahoman*	2
	1	*Tulsa World*	
5. *California Division of Labor Standards Enforcement v. Dillingham Construction*	2(1)	*Los Angeles Times*	0
	1	*Fresno Bee*	
	1	*San Francisco Examiner*	
	2(1)	*Sacramento Bee*	
6. *Chandler v. Miller*	5(1)	*Atlanta Journal Constitution*	2
	1(1)	*Augusta Chronicle*	
7. *General Motors Corp. v. Tracy, Tax Comm'r of Ohio*	1	*Columbus Dispatch*	0
	1	*Dayton Daily News*	
	1	*Plain Dealer*	
	1	*Cincinnati Enquirer*	
8. *Idaho v. Coeur D'Alene Tribe*	1	*Spokesman Review (Idaho Edition)*	1
9. *Glickman v. Wileman Brothers & Elliott, Inc.*	1	*Daily News of Los Angeles*	1
	2	*Los Angeles Times*	
	2(1)	*Fresno Bee*	
	1	*Sacramento Bee*	
	1	*Lewiston Morning Tribune*	
	1	*San Francisco Chronicle*	

Case	Local media stories		The New York Times
10. *Inter Modal Rail Employees Assoc. v. Atchison, Topeka & Santa Fe Railway Co.*	1	*Los Angeles Times*	1
11. *Joseph P. Mazurek, Attorney General of Montana v. James H. Armstrong*	na		1
12. *Klehr Et Ux. v. A. O. Smith Corp.*	1	*Star-Tribune*	0
13. *Lindh v. Murphy, Warden*	2	*Milwaukee Journal Sentinel*	0
	1	*Capital Times*	
	1	*Wisconsin State Journal*	
13. *Maryland v. Wilson*	3(1)	*The Baltimore Sun*	1
	1(1)	*The Daily Record*	
14. *O'Dell v. Netherland, Warden*	2	*Roanoke Times and World Report*	5
	3(1)	*Virginian Pilot*	
	3(1)	*Richmond Times Dispatch*	
15. *Printz, Sheriff/Coroner, Ravalli County, Montana v. United States*	na		4(2)
16. *Reno v. Bossier Parish School Board*	1(1)	*Times-Picayune*	1
17. *Richards v. Wisconsin*	3(2)	*Milwaukee Journal Sentinel*	3
	1(1)	*Capitol Times*	
	2	*Wisconsin State Journal*	
18. *Schenck v. Pro Choice Network of Western New York*	7(2)	*Buffalo News*	5(1)
	3(1)	*Times Union*	
19. *Strate v. A-1 Contractors*	0		0
20. *United States v. Alaska*	2(1)	*Anchorage Daily News*	2
21. *United States v. Brockamp, Admin'r of the Estate of McGill, Deceased*	3	*Los Angeles Times*	1
22. *United States v. Lanier*	3(1)	*The Tennessean*	
	3	*Chattanooga Free Press*	
	1(1)	*Commercial Appeal*	
23. *United States v. O'Hagan*	1(1)	*Star Tribune*	1

Note: Information obtained from a search of state newspapers on Academic Universe (a subset of Lexis-Nexis). Number in parentheses indicates the number of front page stories. No media information was available for the state of Montana.

Appendix D

Statistical Issues with the Analysis of Panel Data

The primary data analyzed in this book are collected from a series of panel studies. Since there are some statistical issues with this kind of analysis, I include a brief discussion of those problems and issues in this appendix, but this section is not essential to understand the analysis presented in the empirical chapters. Specifically, there are various concerns with how the dependent variables are measured. In panel studies, there are a number of approaches to analyzing effects over time. Two of the most common groups of approaches are "change score" models and "regression adjustment" or "static score" models (Judd and Kenney 1984; Finkel 1995). Each of these models improves upon standard cross-sectional approaches by incorporating the dynamic components, but in so doing they can suffer from a different set of statistical problems.

The "change score" method uses simple differences between the level of the dependent variable at the various time points. In a two-wave study, the change score is simply the difference between the dependent variable at the first and second measurements. This method regresses the change in Y on the change in X. Variations in this general model include using either X from a single time point rather than the change in X. This model is also known as the "unconditional change score" or the method of first differences (Finkel 1995, pg. 5). The key characteristic of this model is that the dependent variable is the difference between the two time points and it is *not* included as an independent variable. Essentially, this model is more concerned with predicting or explaining *change*, rather than predicting or explaining the *absolute level* of the dependent variable at the second time point. A particular advantage of this type of analysis of panel data, as opposed to the types discussed below, is that it controls for problems associated with omitted variables. When certain relatively stable traits are not included in the model, their absence does not bias the estimates of the model as it would in a cross-sectional study. In the cross-sectional study, the bias is caused because the effect of these omitted variables is included in the error term. In the change score model, the effect disappears through differencing (Finkel 1995).

Though this model seems straightforward, there are also some short-comings. Most notably, this specification may suffer from regression to the mean effects. Regression to the mean is simply the tendency for ex-treme values of a variable at one time point to become less extreme at subsequent measurements. In other words, there tends to be a negative correlation between initial values of variable and the values measured subsequently.

Regression to the mean can occur for a number of reasons. A major portion of the problem is associated with random measurement error in the dependent variable. But, even with perfect measurement, panel stud-ies can suffer from regression effects. As Finkel notes, "extreme scores on Y_{t-1} are caused in part by large error terms that represent the effects of all omitted variables as well as purely random factors. Therefore, change in Y may be negatively related to Y_{t-1}, as the error terms will tend to be smaller in the subsequent measurements. If this is the case, then omit-ting Y_{t-1} can lead to a downward bias in the estimated effect on Y *of any independent variable X that is positively related to both Y_t and Y_{t-1}*" (Finkel 1995, 8; emphasis mine). This last point will be expanded upon below.

The other main type of analysis is the regression adjustment approach (Judd and Kenny 1981). This model is distinguished from the above model by the inclusion of Y_{t-1} as an *independent* variable as well. In this model, Y_{t-1} is included as an independent variable in order to help control for prior levels of the dependent variable. This model is also called the "static score" or "conditional change" model (Finkel 1995, pg. 6) In this model, Y_{t-1}, the value of the independent variable at the initial measurement is used to help explain the level of the variable at the second measurement. Some researchers suggest it as a better alternative to the change score model described above because it is less susceptible to problems associated with regression effects. This model is somewhat different substantively as well. Rather than predicting the *change* between the initial value and the subsequent value, this model predicts the *level* of the variable at the second wave by using the initial value as an explanatory variable. Another difference between this type of model and the change score model is that this model will always explain a greater portion of the variance in the level of the dependent variable simply by including Y_{t-1}.

A modification of this model expresses the dependent variable in terms of the change between the measurements by subtracting Y_{t-1} from the equation. With this model, it is possible to predict or explain the *change* in the dependent variable while controlling for the initial value of the dependent variable. This model is different from the previous model since the effect of Y_{t-1} in this model is the same as the effect of Y_{t-1} in the previous model *minus* one. The critical assumption of this model is that the effect of Y_{t-1} is constant over time.

There is no definitive criterion for determining which model to adopt since there are benefits and drawbacks to both. For the purposes of this book, the third model appears to offer the most advantages and minimizes the disadvantages. The questions posed in this book are less about explaining the absolute level of support for particular policies and evaluation of the Court than they are about how Court decisions *change* these attitudes.

References

Abraham, Henry J., and Barbara A. Perry. 1998. *Freedom and the Court: Civil Rights and Liberties in the United States.* 7th Ed. New York: Oxford University Press.

Adamany, David. 1973. "Legitimacy, Realigning Elections, and the Supreme Court." *Wisconsin Law Review.* 3: 790–846.

Adamany, David, and Joel B. Grossman. 1983. "Support for the Supreme Court as a National Policymaker." *Law & Policy Quarterly.* 5 (October): 405–37.

Baker v. Carr. 1962. 369 U.S. 186.

Bass, Larry R., and Dan Thomas. 1984. "The Supreme Court and Policy Legitimation: Experimental Tests." *American Politics Quarterly.* 12: (July): 335–60.

Berkson, Larry C. 1978. *The Supreme Court and Its Publics: The Communication of Policy Decisions.* Lexington, Mass.: Lexington Books.

Board of Airport Commissioners v. Jews for Jesus. 1987. 482 U.S. 569.

Board of Education of Kiryas Joel Village School District v. Grumet. 1994. 512 U.S. 687.

Board of Education of Westside Comm. Schools v. Mergens. 1990. 496 U.S. 226.

Boninger, David S., Matthew K. Berent, and Jon A. Krosnick. 1995. "Origins of Attitude Importance: Self-Interest, Social Identification, and Value Relevance." *Journal of Personality and Social Psychology.* 68 (January): 61–80.

Boy Scouts of America v. Dale. 2000. 530 U.S. 640.

Bray v. Alexandria Women's Health Clinic. 1993. 506 U.S. 263.

Brown v. Board of Education of Topeka, Kansas. 1954. 347 U.S. 483.

Brown v. Board of Education of Topeka, Kansas. 1955. 349 U.S. 294.

Bruce Babbitt, Secretary of the Interior, et al., v. Sweet Home Chapter of Communities for a Great Oregon, et al. 1995. 515 U.S. 687.

Bush v. Gore. 2000. 530 U.S. 98.

Caldeira, Gregory A. 1986. "Neither the Purse nor the Sword: Dynamics of Public Confidence in the Supreme Court." *American Political Science Review.* 80 (December): 1209–26.

Caldeira, Gregory A. 1991. "Courts and Public Opinion." In *The American Courts.* Ed. John B. Gates and Charles A. Johnson. Washington, D.C.: CQ Press.

Caldeira, Gregory A., and James L. Gibson. 1992. "Etiology of Public Support for the United States Supreme Court." *American Journal of Political Science.* 36 (August): 635–64.

Canon, Bradley C., and Charles A. Johnson. 1999. *Judicial Policies: Implementation and Impact.* 2d ed. Washington, D.C.: CQ Press.

Capital Square Review and Advisory Bard v. Pinette. 1995. 505 U.S. 753.

Casey, Gregory. 1974. "The Supreme Court and Myth." *Law and Society Review.* 8 (Spring): 385–419.

Casper, Jonathan D. 1976. "The Supreme Court and National Policy Making." *American Political Science Review.* 70 (March): 50–63.

Choper, Jesse. 1980. *Judicial Review and the National Political Process.* Chicago: University of Chicago Press.

Cipollone v. Liggett. 1992. 505 U.S. 504.

City of Boerne v. Flores. 1997. 521 U.S. 507.

Dahl, Robert. 1957. "Decision Making in a Democracy: The Supreme Court as a National Policy Maker." *Journal of Public Law.* 6 (Fall): 279–95.

Davis, James A., Tom W. Smith, and Peter V. Marsden. 1998. *General Social Surveys, 1972–1998 [Cumulative File].*[Computer file]. 3rd version. Chicago, IL: National Opinion Research Center [producer]. Storrs, CT: Roper Center for Public Opinion Research, University of Connecticut/Ann Arbor, MI: Inter-university Consortium for Political and Social Research [distributors].

Davis, Richard. 1994. *Decisions and Images. The Supreme Court and the Press.* Englewood Cliffs, NJ: Prentice-Hall.

Dolbeare, Kenneth M. 1967. "The Public Views the Supreme Court," in Herbert Jacob (ed), *Law, Politics, and the Federal Courts.* Boston: Little-Brown.

Dolbeare, Kenneth M., and Phillip E. Hammond. 1968. "The Political Party Basis of Attitudes Toward the Supreme Court." *Public Opinion Quarterly.* 32 (Spring):16–30.

Durr, Robert H., Andrew D. Martin, and Christina Wolbrecht. 2000. "Ideological Divergence and Public Support for the Supreme Court." *American Journal of Political Science.* 44 (October): 768–76.

Easton, David. 1965. *A Systems Analysis of Political Live.* New York: Wiley.

Easton, David. 1975. "Reassessment of Concept of Political Support." *British Journal of Political Science.* 5 (October): 435–57.

Easton, David, and Jack Dennis. 1969. *"Children in the Political System: Origins of Political Legitimacy."* New York: McGraw-Hill.

Finkel, Steve. 1995. *Causal Analysis with Panel Data.* Sage University Paper on Quantitative Applications in Social Science, 07-105. CA.

Fiske, Susan, and Shelly Taylor. 1991. *Social Cognition.* 2d ed. McGraw-Hill, Inc.

Flemming, Roy B., and B. Dan Wood. 1997. "The Public and the Supreme Court: Individual Justice Responsiveness to American Policy Moods." *American Journal of Political Science.* 41 (April): 468–98.

Flemming, Roy B., John Bohte, and B. Dan Wood. 1997. "One Voice Among Many: The Supreme Court's Influence on Attentiveness to Issues in the United

States, 1947–1992." *American Journal of Political Science.* 41 (October): 1224–50.

Franklin, Charles, and Liane C. Kosaki. 1989. "Republican Schoolmaster: The U.S. Supreme Court, Public Opinion, and Abortion." *American Political Science Review.* 83 (September): 751–71.

Franklin, Charles, and Liane C. Kosaki. 1995. "Media, Knowledge, and Public Evaluations of the Supreme Court." In *Contemplating Courts.* Ed. Lee J. Epstein. CQ Press, Washington, D.C.

Franklin, Charles, Liane C. Kosaki, and Herbert Kritzer. 1993. "The Salience of United States Supreme Court Decisions." Paper presented at the annual meeting of the American Political Science Association, Washington, D.C.

Gibson, James L. 1989. "Understandings of Justice: Institutional Legitimacy, Procedural Justice, and Political Tolerance." *Law and Society Review.* 25 (August): 631–6.

Gibson, James L., and Gregory A. Caldeira. 1992. "Blacks and the United States Supreme Court: Models of Diffuse Support." *Journal of Politics.* 54 (November): 1120–45.

Gibson, James L., Gregory A. Caldeira, and Vanessa Baird. 1998. "On the Legitimacy of National High Courts." *American Political Science Review.* 92 (June): 343–58.

Gibson, James L., Gregory A. Caldeira, and Lester Kenyatta Spence. 2001. "The Supreme Court and the U.S. Presidential Election of 2000: Wounds, Self-Inflicted or Otherwise?" Working Paper #182. The Russell Sage Foundation.

Graber, Doris. 1997. *Mass Media and American Politics.* 5th ed.. Washington, D.C.: CQ Press.

Grosskopf, Anke, and Jeffrey J. Mondak. 1998. "Do Attitudes Toward Specific Supreme Court Decisions Matter? The Impact of Webster and Texas v. Johnson on Public Confidence in the Supreme Court." *Political Research Quarterly.* 51 (September):633–54.

Handberg, Roger. 1984. "Public Opinion and the United States Supreme Court, 1935–1981." *International Social Science Review.* 59 (Winter): 3–13.

Handberg, Roger, and William S. Maddox. 1982. "Public Support for the Supreme Court in the 1970s." *American Politics Quarterly.* 10 (July): 333–46.

Hibbing, John R., and Elizabeth Theiss-Morse. 1995. *Congress as Public Enemy: Public Attitudes Toward American Political Institutions.* New York: Cambridge University Press.

Hill v. Colorado. 2000. 530 U.S. 703.

Hochschild, Jennifer L. 1984. *The New American Dilemma.* New Haven: Yale University Press.

Hoekstra, Valerie J. 1995. "The Supreme Court and Opinion Change: An Experimental Study of the Court's Ability to Change Opinion." *American Politics Quarterly.* 23 (January): 109–29.

Hoekstra, Valerie J. 2000. "The Supreme Court and Local Public Opinion." *American Political Science Review.* 94 (March): 89–100.

Hoekstra, Valerie J., and Jeffrey A. Segal. 1996. "The Shepherding of Local Public Opinion: The Supreme Court and *Lamb's Chapel.*" *The Journal of Politics.* 58 (November): 1079–1102.

ISKCON v. Lee. 1992. 505 U.S. 672.

Iyengar, Shanto. 1991. *Is Anyone Responsible? How Television Frames Political Issues.* Chicago: University of Chicago Press.

Iyengar, Shanto, Mark D. Peters, and Donald S. Kinder. 1982. "Experimental Demonstrations of the 'Not-so-Minimal' Consequences of Television News Programs." *American Political Science Review.* 76 (December): 848–58.

Jaros, Dean, and Robert Roper. 1980. "The United States Supreme Court" Myth, Diffuse Support, Specific Support, and Legitimacy." *American Politics Quarterly.* 8 (January): 85–105.

Johnson, Timothy R., and Andrew D. Martin. 1998. "The Public's Conditional Response to Supreme Court Decisions." *American Political Science Review.* 92 (June): 299–309.

Kaniss, Phyllis. 1991. *Making Local News.* Chicago, Il.: University of Chicago Press.

Katsh, Ethan. 1983. "The Supreme Court Beat: How Television Covers the Supreme Court." *Judicature.* 67 (June/July): 6–12.

Kessel, John. 1966. "Public Perceptions of the Supreme Court." *Midwest Journal of Political Science.* 10 (May): 167–91.

Kritzer, Herbert M. 2001. "The Impact of *Bush v. Gore* on Public Perceptions and Knowledge of the Supreme Court." *Judicature.* 85 (July/August): 32–38.

Krosnick, Jon A., David Boninger, and Yao Chuang. 1993. "Attitude Strength: One Construct or Many Related Constructs?" *Journal of Personality and Social Psychology.* 65 (December): 1132–51.

Lamb's Chapel v. Center Moriches Free Union School District 1993. 508 U.S. 384.

Larkin v. Grendel's Den, Inc. 1982. 459 U.S. 116.

Lemon v. Kurtzman. 1971. 403 U.S. 602.

Lodge, Milton, Kathleen M. McGraw, and Patrick Stroh. "An Impression-Driven Model of Candidate Evaluation." *American Political Science Review.* 83 (June): 399–419.

Lodge, Milton, Marco R. Steenbergen, and Shawn Brau. 1995. "The Responsive Voter: Campaign Information and the Dynamics of Candidate Evaluation." *American Political Science Review.* 89 (June): 309–326.

Lynch v. Donnelly. 1984. 465 U.S. 668.

Lyons, John M., and William Scheb. 2000. "The Myth of Legality and Public Evaluation of the Supreme Court." *Social Science Quarterly.* 81 (December): 928–40.

Madsen et al., v. Women's Health Center Inc., et al. 1994. 512 U.S. 753.

Marcus, George, and Michael MacKuen. 1993. "Anxiety, Enthusiasm, and the Vote: The Emotional Underpinnings of Learning and involvement During Presidential Campaigns." *American .Political Science Review.* 87 (June): 672–85.

Markus, Gregory. 1990. *Analysis of Panel Data.* Sage University Paper on Quantitative Applications in Social Science, 07-018. CA.

Marshall, Thomas. 1988. "Public Opinion, Representation, and the Modern Supreme Court." *American Politics Quarterly.* 16: 296–316.

Marshall, Thomas. 1989. *Public Opinion and the Supreme Court.* Unwin Hyman, Inc. Boston, MA.

Mishler, William, and Reginald S. Sheehan. 1993. "The Supreme Court as a Counter-majoritarian Institution? The Impact of Public Opinion on Supreme Court Decisions." *American Political Science Review.* 87 (March):87–101.

Mishler, William, and Reginald S. Sheehan. 1996. "Public Opinion, the Attitudinal Model, and Supreme Court Decision Making: A Micro- Analytic Perspective." *The Journal of Politics.* 58 (February): 169–200.

Mitchell v. Helms. 2000. 530 U.S. 793.

Mondak, Jeffery J. 1990. "Perceived Legitimacy of Supreme Court Decisions: Three Functions of Source Credibility." *Political Behavior.* 12 (December): 363–84.

Mondak, Jeffery J. 1991. "Substantive and Procedural Aspects of Supreme Court Decisions as Determinants of Approval." *American Politics Quarterly.* 19 (April):174–88.

Mondak, Jeffery J. 1992. "Institutional Legitimacy, Policy Legitimacy, and the Supreme Court." *American Politics Quarterly.* 20 (October): 457–77.

Mondak, Jeffery J. 1994. Policy Legitimacy and the Supreme Court: The Sources and Contexts of Legitimation. *Political Research Quarterly.* 47 (September): 675–92.

Mondak, Jeffery J. 1995. *Nothing to Read: Newspapers and Elections in a Social Experiment.* Ann Arbor: University of Michigan Press.

Mondak, Jeffery J., and Shannon Ishiyama Smithey. 1997. "The Dynamics of Public Support for the Supreme Court." *The Journal of Politics.* 59 (November): 1114–42.

Muir, William K., Jr. 1973. *Law and Attitude Change.* Chicago: University of Chicago Press.

Murphy, Walter F., and Joseph Tanenhaus. 1968a. "Public Opinion and the Supreme Court: The Goldwater Campaign." *Public Opinion Quarterly.* 32 (Spring):31.

Murphy, Walter F., and Joseph Tanenhaus. 1968b. "Public Opinion and the U.S. Supreme Court: Mapping of Some Prerequisites for Court Legitimation of Regime Changes." *Law and Society Review.* 2 (May): 357–82.

Murphy, Walter F., and Joseph Tanenhaus. 1972. *The Study of Public Law.* New York: Random House.

Newland, Chester. 1964. "Press Coverage of the United States Supreme Court." *Western Political Quarterly.* 19 (March): 15–36.

Norpoth, Helmut, and Jeffrey A. Segal. 1994. "Popular Influence on Supreme Court Decisions." *American Political Science Review.* 88 (September): 711–16.

O'Brien, David M. 1986. *Storm Center: The Supreme Court in American Politics.* New York: W. W. Norton & Company.

Oklahoma Tax Commission v. Chickasaw Nation. 1995. 515 U.S. 450.

Pacelle, Richard L. 1991. *The Transformation of the Supreme Court's Agenda: From the New Deal to the Reagan Administration.* Boulder, Colo.: Westview Press, 1991.

Petty, Richard F., and John T. Cacioppo. 1986. "The Elaboration Likelihood Model of Persuasion." In *Advances in Experimental Social Psychology.* (Volume 19). Ed. L. Berkowitz. New York, NY: Academic Press.

Planned Parenthood of Southeastern Pennsylvania v. Casey. 1992. 505 U.S. 833.

Quill Corp. v. North Dakota. 1992. 504 U.S. 298.

R.A.V. v. City of St. Paul. 1992. 505 U.S. 377.

Rehnquist, William H. 1999. "On Doing the Right Thing and Giving Public Satisfaction." *Court Review: The Journal of the American Judges Association.* 36 (Fall): 8–9.

Roe v. Wade. 1973. 410 U.S. 113.

Rosenberg, Gerald. 1991. *The Hollow Hope: Can Courts Bring about Social Change?* Chicago: University of Chicago Press.

Rosenberger v. Rector and Visitors of University of Virginia. 1995. 505 U.S. 819.

Santa Fe Independent School District v. Doe. 2000. 530 U.S. 290.

Schenck v. Pro-Choice Network of Wester New York. 1997. 519 U.S. 357.

Sears, David O. 1986. "College Sophomores in the Laboratory: Influences of a Narrow Data Base on Social Psychology's View of Human Nature." *Journal of Personality and Social Psychology.* 51 (September): 515–30.

Segal, Jeffrey A., and Harold J. Spaeth 1993. *The Supreme Court and the Attitudinal Model.* New York: Cambridge University Press.

Segal, Jennifer A. 1995. "Diffuse Support for the United States Supreme Court: Reliable Reservoir or Fickle Foundation?" Paper presented at the annual meeting of the Midwest Political Science Association, Chicago, Il.

Sigelman, Lee. 1979. "Black-White Differences in Attitudes Toward the Supreme Court.: A Replication in the 1970s." *Social Science Quarterly.* 60 (June): 113–19.

Slotnick, Elliot E., and Jennifer A. Segal. 1998. *Television News and the Supreme Court: All the News that's Fit to Air?* New York: Cambridge University Press.

Slotnick, Elliot E., Jennifer A. Segal, and Lisa M. Compoli. 1994. "Television News and the Supreme Court: Correlates of Decisional Coverage." Paper presented at the Annual Meeting of the American Political Science Association, New York, NY.

Spaeth, Harold J. 1998. United States Supreme Court Judicial Data Base, 1953–1996 terms. 8th ed. Ann Arbor, MI: Inter-University Consortium for Political and Social Research.

Sternberg, et al., v. Carhart. 2000. 530 U.S. 914.

Stimson, James A., Michael B. MacKuen, and Robert S. Erikson. 1995. "Dynamic Representation." *American Political Science Review.* 89 (September): 543–65.

Tanenhaus, Joseph, and Walter Murphy. 1981. "Patterns of Public Support for the Supreme Court: A Panel Study." *The Journal of Politics.* 43 (February): 24–39.

Texas v. Johnson. 1989. 491 U.S. 397.

Troxel v. Granville. 2000. 530 U.S. 57.

United States v Kokinda. 1990. 497 U.S. 720.

United States Bureau of the Census. 1990. *Census on Population and Housing, 1990.* Bureau of the Census. Washington, D.C.

Vacco v. Quill. 1997. 521 U.S. 793.

Washington v. Glucksberg. 1997. 521 U.S. 702.

Webster v. Reproductive Health Services.

Wyer, Robert S., Robert S. Budesheim, Thomas Lee, and Sharon Shavitt. 1991. "Image, Issues, and Ideology: The Processing of Information about Political Candidates." *Journal of Personality and Social Psychology.* 61 (October): 533–45.

Zobrest v. Catalina Foothills School District. 1993. 509 U.S. 1.

Index

Page numbers in italics refer to tables

2000 Election, *1, 2*, 51. *See also Bush v. Gore*

ABC, 57. *See also* media coverage of the Supreme Court, television
Abraham, Henry J., 41n10
Ada Evening News, The, 61, 66, 67, 81. *See also* media coverage of the Supreme Court
Adamany, David, 17, 120, 126
Ada, Oklahoma, 8, 42–6; aftermath of Supreme Court's decision, 45; background of dispute, 54; imposition of gasoline taxes, 44; income tax, 42n14; Native Americans, 42–5, 43nn15, 16; prior disputes 42–4, 63. *See also Oklahoma Tax Commission v. Chickasaw Nation*
agenda setting. *See* media coverage of the Supreme Court
aggregate data: versus individual data, *3, 4, 9, 10, 12, 13,* 23–4, 55, 118, 145, 147, 152; and changes in public opinion, 90, 92, 94; and support for the Court, 12, 116–18, 124–8. *See also* awareness of the Supreme Court; cross-sectional

surveys; Supreme Court and public opinion, support for the Supreme Court
Albany Democrat Herald, 61, 62, 67nd, 81. *See also* media coverage of the Supreme Court
Alfred P. Murrah Federal Building: bombing of, 27n2, 63, 76
American Center for Law and Justice, 36–7, 36n3. *See also Lamb's Chapel v. Center Moriches Union Free School District*
American Jewish Congress, 40. *See also Board of Education of Kiryas Joel v. Grumet*
Associated Press (AP), 65, 66. *See also* media coverage of the Supreme Court
attention to the Supreme Court. *See* awareness of Supreme Court decisions; media coverage of the Supreme Court
awareness of Supreme Court decisions, 6–7, 72–82, 119, 150–1; attention to politics/media and, 7, 52, 73–5, 78–82, 151; education effects and, 7, 78–82, 151; in immediate and surrounding